GOOD GRuB

Making the Most of the Garden's Edible Gifts

Compiled and Edited by

Jennifer Grant & Linda Bondurant

A Collection of Recipes from GRuB

GRuB (Garden-Raised Bounty)
2016 Elliott Avenue NW
Olympia WA 98502

360.753.5522
goodgrub.org
facebook.com/GRuB.WA
twitter.com/GRuBinOly

Copyright © 2012 GRuB
All Rights Reserved

ISBN-10: 1477565590
ISBN-13: 978-1477565599

DEDICATION

This cookbook is dedicated to all of the youth and gardeners who share their energy, creativity, and compassion with us year after year. This is an old story, this is a new story, this is the same story; different than before. Thank you to all those who make our work possible.

APPRECIATION

As a food-growing organization, we give thanks to indigenous peoples worldwide who for thousands of years have been the stewards of the seeds that become the foods and medicines that nourish all of us. May our work honor the Squaxin Tribe, on whose land our farm now sits, and Bonnie Turner, whose legacy of kind-hearted generosity allows this work to flourish. Bonnie was an avid gardener who opened her space to our work in 1996. She watched our program grow and her legacy continued after her passing, thanks to the generosity of granddaughter Linda Newcomb, who offered GRuB the opportunity to purchase the land, a 2-acre parcel that is now the GRuB Farm.

ACKNOWLEDGEMENTS

The recipes in this cookbook came to us from our wonderful GRuB supporters and volunteers. Our special thanks to the following for sharing favorite recipes, many of which are old family favorites: Linda Bondurant, Virginia Drake Cocayne, Mike Extine, Jennifer Grant, Jim Grant, Joanne Lee, Ingrid Lundin, Steve Lundin, Erin Majors, Kathleen Moore, Sharon Rahm, Liza Rognas, and Sage Van Zandt. Thank you also to Olympia spice shop owner, Anne Buck, of Buck's Fifth Avenue (culinaryexotica@gmail.com), for her support of our culinary efforts. A big thank you to GRuB staffer, Anna Robinson, for her help with the cover design. And to Jim Wark we give special thanks for sharing his expertise in photo editing, so we could make sure the photographs met publication standards.

USING THIS COOKBOOK

The recipes in this cookbook are arranged by food category rather than the usual listings of appetizers, salads, and soups and such. The intent is to give the cook a quick and easy way to find a recipe when the harvest has given one excess kale, tomatoes, or zucchini. So often the good foods harvested go to waste for lack of inspiring recipes or ways to use them. The recipes have been tagged, as well, for cooks looking for special kinds of recipes:

QE means a recipe is quick and easy. There are minimal ingredients, all readily available. Preparation is simple and cooking/baking time usually an hour or less.

VG means a recipe is vegetarian; it contains no meat, fish, or poultry. Some recipes contain eggs or dairy products such as cheese, cream, etc. Strict vegetarians and vegans will need to make adjustments or ingredient substitutions.

GF means a recipe is gluten free; it contains no wheat, barley, rye, or oats.

DF means a recipe is free of milk or milk products; it contains no milk, cheese, yogurt, or other types of milk products.

CONTENTS

Introduction	7
Bulbs, Roots & Tubers	9
. onions . garlic . leeks . carrots . parsnips . beets . turnips. rutabagas .	
. potatoes . sweet potato .	
Brassicas	32
. kale . cabbage . cauliflower . broccoli . Brussels sprouts . kohlrabi .	
Corn, Peas, Beans, & Pods	57
. corn . shelling peas . pea pods . green beans . lima beans .	
Legumes & Grains	73
. dried beans . dried peas . lentils . barley. bulgur . polenta . quinoa . oats .	
Shoots & Stems	88
. asparagus . fennel . rhubarb .	
Squash	98
. summer squash . winter squash . pumpkin .	
Fruiting Vegetables	115
. tomatoes . peppers . eggplant . cucumber . globe artichokes .	
Leaves & Greens	135
. lettuce . greens . chard . spinach .	
Fruits, Nuts & Seeds	147
. apples . pears . cherries . berries . sunflower seeds . pumpkin . seeds .	
Herbs & Edible Flowers	161
. basil . cilantro . parsley . dill . mint . chives . bee balm . tarragon . thyme .	
. rosemary . sage. oregano . marjoram . lavender . calendula . nasturtium .	
Gifts from the Garden	173
The Cook's Helpers	177
. culinary terms . recipe abbreviations . weights & measures . metrics .	
. food equivalencies . substitutions . the well-stocked pantry .	
Index: Recipes by Garden Ingredient	188
Index: Recipes by Meal Item	201

"I love bringing good food home...working at GRuB has influenced me to eat much healthier foods and to be more active."

– Cultivating Youth Crewmember

"I wanted a garden for the ability to grow natural food and to teach my daughter how to grow her own food as well."

– Kitchen Garden Project Gardener

INTRODUCTION

Welcome to Backyard Gardening and Home Cooking!

At GRuB, we believe that **good food is a basic human right**. Growing, eating and gathering around healthy food is a simple and powerful way to connect people to each other and to important work in our community.

We hope you, your family, and your neighbors see your garden as the beginning of a new way to build connections with one another. As your seeds sprout and grow into hearty vegetables and you harvest the fruits of your labor together, you can look forward to cooking delicious meals using some of the fabulous recipes we've compiled in this cookbook.

Happy Cooking!

Love,
GRuB and Jennifer & Linda *(pictured below with the Rhubarb Walnut Bread on pg. 94!)*

GRuB's Vision.....

We envision a world where everyone has a place at the table;
Everyone is nourished by healthy, sustainably grown food;
Everyone has a sense of belonging; and
Everyone is an inspired and honored contributor to our community.

GRuB's Mission

Our mission is to inspire positive personal and community change by bringing people together around food and agriculture. To fulfill this mission we partner with youth and low-income families to create empowering individual and community food solutions by offering activities, trainings, tools and resources to help build a just and sustainable food system.

We work in Thurston and Mason counties in the South Puget Sound region of Washington State.

GOOD GRuB Recipes

Bulbs, Roots, & Tubers

Basic Ways of Cooking & Serving

Vegetable	Preparation	Cooking Time	Ways to Serve
Beets	Scrub clean; remove leafy tops. To cook, leave whole. After cooking, drain, run cold water over the beets and slip off the skins and root end.	Boil in salted water for 30-45 minutes or until tender. Add a little vinegar to the cooking water to preserve color.	Buttered with salt and pepper. Vary with fresh garden herbs - dill, savory, thyme, marjoram or grated orange or lemon rind.
Carrots	Remove tops; scrub; pare thin or scrape. Leave whole or cut into "coins," cubes or sticks.	Steam in a saucepan until tender, about 10 minutes.	Buttered with salt and pepper. Vary with fresh garden herbs - parsley, basil, savory, thyme, mint.
Garlic	Peel, mince for use as an ingredient. Leave whole to bake.	Sauté in cooking oil to release flavor. Watch so garlic doesn't brown too much or burn. To bake, rub garlic head with oil; wrap in foil. Bake at 350° 30 minutes or until garlic is soft. Squeeze cloves to release soft garlic.	Add as an ingredient to casseroles or in stir fry, scramble, or sauté dishes. Use baked garlic in garlic mashed potatoes, as an appetizer on bread or crackers, or as an ingredient in other recipes.
Onions - yellow	Peel under running water (to prevent tears). Leave whole, slice, quarter or chop based on intended use.	Bake whole at 350° for 50-60 minutes; boil whole 30-40 minutes; sauté in cooking oil about 5 minutes, until tender.	Buttered with salt and pepper. Vary with fresh garden herbs - thyme, basil. Use as an ingredient in other dishes.
Parsnip	Pare or scrub with a brush. Leave whole or cut in "coins" or cubes.	Boil whole 20-40 minutes, pieces 8-20 minutes. Bake at 350° 30-45 minutes.	Buttered with salt and pepper. Vary with fresh minced parsley. Mashed; as an ingredient in soup.
Potatoes	Scrub with brush. Remove eyes. Leave skin on whenever possible. Cut in large pieces or leave whole to bake.	Boil 20-25 minutes. Bake at 350° for 1 to 1 ½ hours. Be sure to poke holes in potato before baking to allow steam to escape.	Buttered with salt and pepper. Vary with fresh herbs - parsley, sauces, condiments. Also mashed.
Rutabagas	Pare, slice, dice, or cut into strips.	Boil 25-40 minutes. Adding a little sugar to the water improves flavor.	Buttered with salt and pepper. Mashed; as an ingredient in soup.
Sweet Potatoes	Boil without paring. When tender, drain and slip off skins. If baking, scrub, then dry.	Boil 30-35 minutes. Bake at 350° 50-60 minutes. Rub with a little cooking oil before baking.	Baked with butter, salt, and pepper. Also mashed.
Turnips	Remove tops. Pare, slice, dice, or cut into strips.	Boil whole 20-30 minutes; sliced, diced, strips 15-20 minutes.	Buttered with salt and pepper. Mashed with cream and nutmeg. Vary with chives.

ⓘ **Tip:** when boiling vegetables, don't drown them in water. Using a small amount (1-2 inches) will help preserve the nutrients. Keep an eye on them so they don't boil dry. Don't throw your cooking water down the drain! Use it later in soups.

ⓘ **Tip:** keep root vegetables (potatoes, beets, onions carrots) in a cool, dry, well-ventilated place.

Now Add Some Creativity!

Creamy Carrot Soup VG GF   Serves 6

2 T. oil
1 medium onion, chopped
2 T. white wine (optional)
4 C. carrots, peeled and thinly sliced
2 C. vegetable stock (recipe for homemade can be found in this chapter)
1 tsp. salt
Pepper to taste
Pinch of nutmeg
1¼ C. milk
2 tsp. fresh chives or parsley, chopped
Sour cream (optional)

Heat oil in a large saucepan over medium-high heat. Add onion and sauté for 5 minutes. Add wine (or substitute the equivalent amount of vegetable stock) and carrots and cook for 1 minute until liquid evaporates. Add stock, salt, pepper, and nutmeg. Bring to a boil, then reduce to simmer for 20 minutes. Purée using an immersion blender or food processor. Add milk while puréeing. If using a food processor, return puréed soup to the saucepan and heat to serving temperature.

Serve in soup bowls with a dollop of sour cream or a sprinkling of chives or parsley.

ⓘ **Information:** carrots provide rich amounts of nutrients such as vitamins A, C, K, and B vitamins, as well as the mineral magnesium. They are also rich in fiber.

Sautéed Carrots    Serves 6

1 T. butter
1 T. olive oil
4½ C. diagonally sliced carrots
6 T. water
¼ tsp. salt
½ tsp. ground pepper
2 T. fresh small sage leaves

Melt butter in a large skillet over medium heat. Add oil to the butter and swirl to coat. Add carrots and water. Lower heat, partially cover and cook 10 minutes until carrots are almost tender. Remove cover; add seasonings and continue cooking on medium-high, stirring frequently, until carrots are tender and lightly browned, about 4 minutes. Sprinkle with sage and serve.

Tip: vary by replacing sage with other fresh herbs from the garden, such as tarragon, marjoram, thyme, parsley, rosemary, mint, lavender flowers.

Carrot Orzo   QE VG   Serves 4

1 - 2 carrots, peeled and cut into 1-inch chunks
2 T. butter
1 C. orzo pasta
1½ C. water
1¼ C. chicken broth (use vegetable stock for vegetarian version)
1 large clove garlic, minced
¼ C. Parmesan cheese
2 T. chopped chives or green onions
1 tsp. minced fresh rosemary

Place carrots in a food processor and chop until fine. Melt butter in medium saucepan over medium heat. Add chopped carrots and orzo, stir-frying until orzo is golden, about 5 minutes. Add water, broth, and garlic; cook uncovered over medium heat until all liquid is absorbed, about 10 minutes. Stir frequently. Stir in remaining ingredients and serve. Season with salt and pepper, if desired.

Orange-Roasted Carrots QE VG GF DF   Serves 4

1½ lbs. carrots, cut diagonally into coins
2 T. olive oil
1 tsp. (packed) finely grated orange peel
1/3 C. orange juice (preferably fresh squeezed)
1½ T. honey
Sea salt
Pepper

Preheat oven to 400°. Arrange carrot coins in a single layer on a rimmed baking sheet. Add 2 tablespoons oil and orange peel; sprinkle with salt and pepper and toss. Pour orange juice over the carrots, then cover tightly with foil. Roast until crisp-tender, about 10 minutes. Remove foil and increase oven to 450°. Drizzle honey over carrots and roast uncovered until carrots are tender and browned in spots, about 10 minutes. Transfer carrots and any juices to serving dish. Drizzle lightly with additional olive oil and sprinkle with sea salt.

Oven-Roasted Carrots and Potatoes QE VG GF   Serves 6

2 lbs. carrots, peeled and halved lengthwise, then crosswise
2 lbs. fingerling potatoes (or Yukon Gold, if fingerlings aren't available)
2 T. olive oil
½ tsp. sea salt
½ tsp. ground black pepper
2 T. minced fresh thyme
½ T. butter

Preheat oven to 400°. Heat a pot of water to boiling over high heat. Do not peel potatoes, but cut in half lengthwise; quarters if larger in size. Boil potatoes until barely tender, about 5 minutes. Drain well, then spread in a single layer on a baking sheet. Add carrots and drizzle with olive oil. Season generously with salt and pepper and gently toss to coat. Bake, stirring occasionally, until potatoes are golden brown, about 20 minutes. Place in a serving bowl and add thyme and butter. Gently toss to coat evenly. Serve warm. Can be made up to 5 hours ahead, then reheated in a 350° oven.

Carrot Cookies VG   Makes 4 dozen

¾ C. butter
¾ C. brown sugar, packed
½ C. granulated sugar
1 egg
1 tsp. vanilla
1¾ C. flour
1 tsp. baking powder
¼ tsp. baking soda
½ tsp. cinnamon
¼ tsp. ground cloves
2 C. oatmeal
1 C. shredded carrots
½ C. raisins or dried cranberries (optional)
½ C. nutmeats (optional)

Preheat oven to 375°. Place butter in mixing bowl and beat with electric mixer until softened. Add the brown sugar, granulated sugar, egg, and vanilla. Beat until fluffy. Combine flour, baking powder, baking soda, cinnamon, and cloves in a separate bowl. Gradually add dry ingredients to the sugar mixture, beating until all has been incorporated. Stir in oats and carrots, as well as any of the optional ingredients desired. Drop by rounded teaspoons two inches apart on an ungreased baking sheet. Bake for 10-12 minutes or until the edges are golden. Cool on racks.

Carrot Loaf QE VG

Makes 2 standard size or 4 mini loaves

3 eggs
1½ C. oil
2 C. sugar
2 C. finely grated carrots
1 small can crushed pineapple, drained
½ C. nuts
3 tsp. vanilla
3 C. flour
1 tsp. soda
1 tsp. salt
3 tsp. cinnamon

Beat together eggs, oil, and sugar. Add remaining ingredients and mix until blended. Pour batter into greased and papered loaf pans. Bake at 325° for 1 hour if using standard size loaf pans; 45 minutes if using mini loaf pans. When done, cool on a rack for ten minutes, then remove from pans. Place loaves on the rack to complete cooling.

Parsnip and Carrot Bake QE VG GF

Serves 4

8 oz. parsnips, peeled and cut into sticks
1 lb. carrots, peeled and cut into sticks
¾ C. vegetable stock   (recipe for homemade can be found in this chapter)
2 T. butter, cut into pieces
½ tsp. salt
Chopped fresh tarragon
Pepper

Heat oven to 375°. Toss all ingredients, except tarragon and pepper together. Place in a greased shallow baking dish. Cover with foil and bake until vegetables are soft, about 45 minutes. Uncover and bake until vegetables brown on top, about 10-15 minutes more. Sprinkle with tarragon and pepper before serving.

Fact: purple, yellow, and red carrots were the only color varieties of carrots cultivated before the 15th or 16th century.

Parsnip Purée

Serves 6

2 lbs. parsnips
½ C. milk
8 T. unsalted butter
Salt

Peel parsnips and boil in salted water until very tender, about 10-15 minutes. Drain in colander. While parsnips are draining, heat milk in a small saucepan. Combine parsnips and milk in a food processor or blender. With motor running, gradually add the butter, making sure it is well mixed and the purée is very smooth. Season lightly with salt. Serve as a side dish or in place of rice or potatoes.

Irish Parsnip and Apple Soup

Serves 6

1 T. butter
1 lb. parsnips, thinly sliced
1 lb. apples, peeled and sliced
1 onion, chopped
2 tsp. curry powder
1 tsp. cumin
1 tsp. coriander
½ tsp. cardamom seeds
1 clove garlic, minced
5 C. vegetable or chicken stock
¾ C. cream
Salt and pepper
Chopped chives or parsley

Heat the butter and when foaming add parsnips, apples and onions. Cook until soft, but not browned. Add the garlic and all the herbs and spices, except chopped chives/parsley. Cook about 2 minutes, stirring constantly. Pour in the stock, stirring until well mixed. Cover and simmer gently for 30 minutes or until parsnips are quite soft. Season with salt and pepper. Purée using an immersion blender or food processor, leaving a bit chunky. If too thick, dilute with a little more stock or water. Add the cream and heat through. Serve with chopped chives or parsley.

Easy Roasted Yellow Potatoes    Serves 4

1 medium onion, roughly chopped
2 T. olive oil
¼ C. fresh parsley, chopped
3 - 4 cl. garlic, minced
1½ lbs. new yellow potatoes such as Yukon Gold, sliced ½-inch thick
1 tsp. salt
Pepper

Heat oven to 425°. Put onion, olive oil, parsley, and garlic in a food processor or blender and purée until smooth. Toss with potatoes and salt, then wrap in foil, crimping to seal. Potatoes should be no more than two layers deep in the foil packet. Bake on a sheet for 45 minutes, until potatoes are tender when poked with a fork. Season with pepper.

Tip: this recipe works just as well on the barbecue grill as it does in the oven.

Sage Roasted Potatoes    Serves 6

2½ lbs. Yukon Gold or similar type potatoes
2 T. olive oil
2 T. minced fresh sage
1 tsp. salt
½ tsp. ground black pepper

Heat oven to 350°. Cut potatoes into ½-inch thick wedges. Dry moisture from potatoes with paper towel. Drizzle potatoes with olive oil, toss to coat. Sprinkle with sage, salt, and pepper. Toss again, then arrange in a single layer on baking sheets. Roast 50-60 minutes, turning occasionally until the potatoes are evenly browned and tender.

Tip: when making mashed potatoes, use applesauce in place of milk. This makes for a very tasty potato dish. Good option for those whose diets are dairy-free.

Fact: the potato is the number one vegetable crop in the world. There are about 100 varieties that range in size, shape, color, starch content, and flavor.

Rosemary New Potatoes   QE VG GF DF   Serves 4

1 lb. small new potatoes
2 T. olive oil
3 sprigs fresh rosemary
Sea salt
Pepper

Heat oven to 375°. Slice potatoes into ½-inch rounds and boil in lightly salted water until crisp-tender, about 7 minutes. Drain and dry well with paper toweling. Heat oil in oven-safe skillet. Add rosemary sprigs and potatoes. Bake without disturbing for 5 minutes. Once potatoes have browned lightly on first side, turn them over and put in oven to finish cooking. Bake 10 minutes. Transfer potatoes to serving platter and season with salt and pepper. Garnish with additional rosemary sprigs.

Cumin Potato Salad   QE VG GF DF   Serves 4

1 lb. baby potatoes (red or other waxy potato)
¼ C. olive oil
2 T. cumin seed
1 large shallot or small red onion, diced
Juice of 1 large lemon, strained
Small bunch parsley, chopped
½ - 2 tsp. kosher salt
Black pepper (fresh ground is best)

Scrub, rinse and cut potatoes so that you have uniform quarters. Boil in salted water till tender, 20 minutes, no more. Drain, but leave potatoes in pot with lid on.

In a saucepan, heat olive oil until hot, but don't let it smoke. Add cumin seed and heat just until fragrant. Add red onion and heat through, but not more than 5 minutes. Pour over potatoes, add lemon juice, and sprinkle with a good amount of freshly ground pepper and kosher salt. Throw in the parsley and toss gently to coat. Serve warm or cold.

**Fact:** potatoes were brought to Europe by Spanish explorers who "discovered" them in South American in the early 16th century. Potatoes have been cultivated in South America for between 4000 and 7000 years.

Fingerling Potatoes with Rosemary   QE VG GF DF   Serves 4

2 lbs. small fingerling potatoes
2 T. extra virgin olive oil
2 T. fresh rosemary leaves
1 tsp. salt

Do not pare or cut potatoes. Boil whole for 12-15 minutes or until tender. Drain and cool slightly. Place potatoes in serving bowl and toss with oil, rosemary, and salt. Serve warm.

Irish Potato and Leek Soup   GF   Serves 6 to 8

4 C. chicken broth (use vegetable stock for a vegetarian version)
3 potatoes, peeled and diced
1½ C. chopped cabbage
1 leek, diced
1 onion, chopped
2 carrots, diced
¼ C. chopped fresh parsley
1 tsp. salt
½ tsp. caraway seeds
½ tsp. pepper
1 bay leaf
½ C. sour cream
1 lb. bacon, cooked and crumbled

Combine all ingredients, except the sour cream and bacon, in a large pot. Heat to boiling, lower to simmer. Cook covered at simmer until all the vegetables are soft. Remove and discard the bay leaf. Combine some of the hot liquid from the pot with sour cream in a small bowl. Mix well, then add back into the pot and stir. Add bacon and stir.

ⓘ**Tip:** this recipe may also be prepared in a slow cooker/crock pot. Follow the same procedure as above, covering and cooking for 8 to 10 hours on low or 4 to 5 hours on high.

ⓘ**Fact:** it is thought that the potato was first brought to the United States in the early 18th century by Irish immigrants who settled in New England.

Old-fashioned Potato Bread VG DF   Makes one 10-inch loaf

1 medium potato
1 (¼-oz.) pkg. active dry yeast
3 T. sugar
2½ tsp. salt
1 C. boiling water
5½ - 6 C. bread flour

Peel and cube the potato; place in a saucepan with enough water to cover and bring to a boil. Cook 20 minutes or until the potato cubes are tender. Drain, reserving ½ cup of the cooking liquid. Set liquid aside to cool to lukewarm (105° to 110°). Add yeast to the lukewarm liquid and stir until dissolved. Let stand 5 minutes until foamy.

Meanwhile, mash the potato cubes and measure out 2/3 cup of the mashed potatoes. In a large mixing bowl combine the 2/3 cup potatoes, the sugar, and salt. Stir in 1 cup boiling water, followed by 2½ cups of flour. Add the yeast mixture to the potato mixture, then cover and let rise in a warm place until nearly doubled in size, about 1 to 1½ hours. Stir down, then stir in as much of the remaining flour as you can. Turn out onto a lightly floured surface and knead in enough remaining flour to make a moderately stiff dough that is smooth and elastic (about 6 to 8 minutes of kneading). Shape into a large round loaf; place on a large greased baking sheet and flatten to a 9-inch diameter. Cover and let rise in a warm place until nearly doubled, about 1 hour. Bake at 375° for 25 minutes or until golden brown.

Potato and Turnip Gratin  Serves 8

2 cl. garlic, minced
2 T. unsalted butter
2½ lbs. new potatoes, peeled and cut into ½-inch cubes
2 lbs. turnips or rutabagas, peeled and cut into ½-inch cubes
4 C. cream
Salt and pepper

Preheat oven to 350°. Grease bottom and sides of a 9-inch square pan with butter. Sprinkle garlic over the pan. Mix potatoes and turnips and arrange in pan. Bring cream to a boil on stove and season with about 2 tsp. salt and 1 teaspoon pepper. Pour over vegetables and cover pan with foil. Bake 30 minutes, uncover, and bake another 20-25 minutes. The vegetables should be very tender and the sauce bubbling and browned on top when done.

Roasted Potato Medley  Serves 6

2 sweet potatoes
4 yellow potatoes (like Yukon Gold)
8 small new potatoes (like fingerling or baby red)
6 T. olive oil
1 T. chopped fresh tarragon (or 1 tsp. dry) or sage leaves
⅛ tsp. salt
⅛ tsp. pepper

Preheat oven to 425°. Peel and cube the sweet potatoes and yellow potatoes. Scrub the new potatoes (do not peel) and cut into cubes. Place in a large saucepan and add enough lightly salted water to cover. Bring to a boil and cook for 3 minutes. Drain thoroughly. Combine potatoes with remaining ingredients and spread in a single layer on a baking sheet. Roast until the potatoes are crisp and browned, about 25 minutes. Serve immediately.

ⓘ **Information:** "white potatoes" are a good source of vitamin C, vitamin B6, copper, potassium, manganese, and dietary fiber.

Cheesy Sweet Potato Mash   VG GF   Serves 8 to 10

6 sweet potatoes (about 3 lbs.)
1½ pkgs. (8-oz size) cream cheese, room temperature
4 T. unsalted butter, cut into pieces, room temperature
Sea salt
Freshly ground pepper
¼ C. mild blue cheese
¼ C. candied pecans or walnuts (store-bought or homemade)

Roast sweet potatoes in a 350° oven on a rimmed baking sheet for about an hour or until tender. Let cool slightly. Remove skins and transfer sweet potatoes to a large saucepan. Add cream cheese and butter, then heat over low heat, mashing until well blended and creamy. Season with salt and pepper. Continue to stir over low heat until hot all the way through. Spoon into a serving dish and garnish with blue cheese crumbles and nuts.

Carolyn's Roasted Sweet Potatoes      Serves 2

2 T. olive oil
1 T. lime juice
1 clove garlic, minced
¼ tsp. cayenne pepper
1 T. spicy mustard
¼ tsp. black pepper
½ tsp. red pepper flakes
1 tsp. chili powder
1 tsp. salt
3 C. sweet potato spears

Preheat oven to 400°. In a large bowl, mix olive oil, lime juice, garlic, and spices. Add sweet potato spears, mix until evenly coated. Arrange in a single layer on a baking sheet and bake for 20 minutes. Turn spears over and continue to bake for 10 minutes more, until crispy and browned. Season with salt and serve.

ⓘ **Information:** sweet potatoes are from a different vegetable family than regular potatoes. They are a good source of potassium, copper and fiber; also protein, calcium and vitamin E.

Sweet Potato Hummus   VG GF DF   Serves 8 to 10

1 lb. sweet potatoes, peeled and diced, boiled until tender and cooled
2 C. cooked chickpeas
¼ C. fresh lemon juice
¼ C. tahini or smooth peanut butter
2 T. olive oil
1 T. cumin, or to taste
1 clove garlic, minced
Salt and black pepper to taste
Lemon zest for garnish
Hot smoked paprika for garnish
Parsley or cilantro for garnish

Crackers, veggies, and/or pita bread to dip.

Whiz everything together, except the garnish ingredients (zest, parsley or cilantro and paprika), in the food processor until smooth. You may need to thin mixture with a bit of water or olive oil. Correct the seasonings to taste. Enjoy!

North African Stew VG GF DF   Serve 6 to 8

1 onion, minced
1 red pepper, minced
2 ribs celery, minced
2 cloves garlic, minced
2 - 3 T. olive oil
2 T. tomato paste (only if using dry blend harissa)
2 - 3 T. harissa, to taste
1 T. cumin, ground
1 T. coriander, ground
1 T. turmeric
1 tsp. cinnamon
2 T. freshly grated ginger
Salt and pepper to taste
3 C. cooked chickpeas
3 lbs. sweet potatoes or yams, peeled and diced
1 bunch of kale, stemmed and chopped
1 qt. stock of choice
1 can diced tomatoes
Lemon juice to taste
Chopped cilantro for garnish
Fresh or fried lemon wedges for garnish

This soup is typically served during Ramadan to break the fast at sundown.

-Linda Bondurant

Sauté onion, red pepper, and celery in olive oil for 3 minutes. Add garlic, tomato paste, harissa, cumin, coriander, cinnamon, turmeric, ginger and cook for 30 seconds. Add sweet potatoes, canned tomatoes, and stock to cover, and bring to a boil. Lower heat to a simmer for 10 minutes. Add chickpeas and kale and cook 5 minutes. Adjust seasonings to taste (salt, pepper, lemon juice). Garnish with cilantro and lemons.

ⓘTip: Harissa comes in both a dry blend and a paste. The dry blend is much less expensive. It is available at Buck's Fifth Avenue spice shop in Olympia, Washington or online at culinaryexotica@gmail.com.

ⓘFact: there are about 400 varieties of sweet potato with flesh color ranging from almost white to purple. Yellow-orange flesh is most common.

Roasted Beets QE VG GF DF   Serves 8

2 lbs. beets, peeled and cut into 1-inch wedges
1 T. olive oil
¼ tsp. ground cinnamon
¼ tsp. salt
Chopped flat-leaf parsley (optional)

Heat oven to 350°. Toss beets with olive oil, cinnamon, and salt. Spread in a single layer on a baking sheet. Roast in the oven until tender, about 1 hour, turning once after 30 minutes. To serve, sprinkle with chopped parsley.

Roasted Beet Salad with Oranges VG GF DF   Serves 6

6 medium beets with greens attached
2 oranges
1 small sweet onion, cut lengthwise in slices
¼ C. red wine vinegar
¼ C. olive oil
2 cloves garlic, minced
½ tsp. grated orange peel

Preheat oven to 400°. Remove the beet greens and chop; set aside. Wrap each beet in foil and place directly on oven rack, roasting until tender, about 1½ hours. Cool, then peel and cut the beets into wedges. Place in a bowl.

Cook beet greens in water just until tender, about 2 minutes. Drain and cool. Squeeze greens to remove excess moisture. Add beet greens to the bowl with beets. Cut peel and white pith from oranges. Working over another bowl and using a sharp knife, cut between membranes to release orange sections. Add orange sections and onion to the bowl with the beet mixture.

Place vinegar, oil, garlic, orange peel, and any orange juice released when sectioning the orange in a screw-top jar and shake vigorously to blend. Add dressing to the beet mixture and toss to coat. Season with salt and pepper. Let stand at room temperature for 1 hour so flavors can blend.

Beets in Mustard Vinaigrette    Serves 4 as a side dish

1 lb. beets, cooked and skins removed, then sliced
¼ C. olive oil
3 T. wine vinegar
3 T. Dijon mustard
1 small onion, chopped fine
Salt & pepper to taste
Crumbled blue cheese (optional)

Place all ingredients except the beets in a screw-top jar. Shake to blend. Pour over beets that have been cooked and sliced. Mix well, then cover and allow to marinate in the refrigerator for at least 24 hours. Before serving, mix well.

To serve, arrange beets on lettuce leaves placed on individual plates and serve as a side dish or salad. Sprinkle with crumbled blue cheese, if desired.

ⓘ **Tip:** these marinated beets can also be used as an ingredient in a fresh garden salad.

Hearty Vegetable Roast    Serves 4

6 C. vegetable chunks - a combination of any of the following: winter squash, sweet potatoes, potatoes, turnips, rutabagas, onion, fennel, carrots, parsnips
1 head of garlic, divided into cloves
Olive oil
Soy sauce
1 C. mushrooms, sliced or whole (if small)
1 T. vinegar
Cayenne and/or black pepper to taste

Preheat oven to 375 - 400°. Place vegetable chunks in a large bowl. Drizzle with olive oil and toss to coat. Spread in a roasting pan and bake for 15 minutes. Remove from oven and stir. Add garlic and sprinkle with the soy sauce and pepper. Bake for another 15 minutes, then remove and stir again. Add mushrooms and sprinkle with vinegar and more pepper. Bake 5 minutes or until the desired doneness is reached.

Roasted Vegetable Ragout VG GF DF   Serves 6

3 medium carrots, sliced
1 large parsnip, peeled and diced
1 large fennel bulb, trimmed and diced
1 large onion, coarsely chopped
10 oz. fresh mushrooms, quartered
1 bell pepper, diced
4 cloves garlic, sliced
2 medium zucchini, diced
2 - 4 tsp. olive oil
2 C. vegetable stock (recipe for homemade can be found in this chapter)
1 (28-oz.) can diced tomatoes in juice
3 tsp. fresh rosemary, chopped
1/3 C. chopped fresh basil
¼ C. chopped fresh flat-leaf parsley
Salt and pepper
Non-stick vegetable oil spray

Pre-heat oven to 400°. Spray rimmed baking sheet with nonstick spray. Spread mushrooms, carrots, onion, bell pepper, fennel, parsnip, and garlic in a single layer on the prepared baking sheet. Drizzle with olive oil; sprinkle with 2 teaspoons rosemary, salt, and pepper. Stirring occasionally, roast until vegetables are tender, about 1 hour.

At this point, add zucchini, 2 cups broth, and tomatoes with juice to the vegetables; stir to blend well. Continue to roast about 30 minutes, until zucchini is tender and juices thicken slightly. Stir occasionally and add more broth if liquid evaporates too quickly.

Transfer ragout to bowl. Mix basil, parsley, and 1 tsp. rosemary into the ragout. Season to taste with salt and pepper.

Serve over rice, pasta, or polenta (see *Polenta with Butter and Cheese* recipe in the Legumes & Grains chapter of this book).

ⓘ**Information:** parsnips provide an excellent source of vitamin C, fiber, folic acid, pantothenic acid, copper, and manganese. They are also a good source of the B vitamins, magnesium, potassium, and vitamin E.

Root Vegetable Pot Pie VG Serves 6 to 8

2 tsp. olive oil
1 leek, sliced into thin half-moons
2 C. red (pearl) onions or 2 C. chopped onion
2 C. peeled, chopped and blanched parsnip
2 C. peeled, chopped and blanched carrots
2 C. peeled, cubed and blanched potatoes
3 T. all-purpose flour
1 tsp. dried chervil
½ tsp. kosher salt
½ tsp. freshly ground black pepper
1½ C. beef broth
¼ C. dry white wine
2 C. shredded Fontina cheese
½ C. + 2 T. heavy whipping cream
Store bought or homemade single pie crust (see pie crust recipe on next page)
1 large egg yolk

Preheat the oven to 350°. Grease a 2-quart baking dish. In a large Dutch oven over medium heat, heat the olive oil. Add leek and sauté for 2 minutes. Add onions, parsnips, carrots, and potato; cook for 4 minutes, stirring occasionally. In a small bowl combine the flour, chervil, salt, and pepper. Add flour mixture to vegetables and stir to coat. Add broth and wine, stirring well to avoid lumps. Bring this mixture to a boil, then add the cheese and ½ cup cream. Simmer about 5 minutes, until mixture thickens then pour into the prepared baking dish. Place the pie crust over the baking dish, sealing and fluting around the edge of the dish. Whisk together the 2 T. of remaining cream and the egg yolk, then brush this onto the pie crust. Using a paring knife, make slits in the center of the dough to allow steam to escape. Bake for 35 to 40 minutes, until the crust is golden brown.

Fact: since they don't rely on weather above ground, a lot of root vegetables have no trouble growing in winter. They can survive in the cold ground or in cold storage, making them invaluable for winter nutrition in cold climates when little else is growing. With the plant's nutrients stored in the root, these vegetables are a powerhouse of vitamins, antioxidants, and complex carbohydrates.

Mom's Pie Crust

Makes 2 crusts

2 C. flour
1 t. salt
1/3 C. butter
1/3 C. shortening

Make a paste of 1/4 cup water and 1/3 cup of flour and salt mixture. Cut shortening and butter into flour until it looks like small peas. Mix in the paste until well blended. Divide into 2 disks. Wrap in plastic and refrigerate for 1 hour. This is a never fail dough. You can roll it out multiple times and it will still be flaky. Easy!

Roasted Vegetables with Chimichurri Sauce

Serves 4

4 sweet potatoes
4 carrots
4 parsnips
2 heads fennel
1 bunch kale
1 can chickpeas (garbanzo beans)
Garlic
Olive oil
Balsamic vinegar
Tamari (soy sauce)
Salt
Pepper
Herbs/spices of your choice - tarragon, coriander, rosemary, etc.
Nutritional yeast (optional)

Heat oven to 375°. Dice or slice the potatoes, carrots, and parsnips and place in a mixing bowl. Add a splash of olive oil, balsamic vinegar, salt, pepper, and desired herbs. Spread on a baking sheet lined with parchment paper. Roast for 45 minutes, stirring once or twice and re-seasoning to taste.

Slice the fennel; splash with olive oil salt and pepper and add to the roasting vegetables during the final 20 to 25 minutes of roasting.

Drain the chickpeas and blot dry. Mix with chopped rosemary (dry will do), chopped garlic, and a splash of olive oil, salt and pepper. Spread on a parchment-lined pan and roast for 30 minutes.

Wash and blot dry the kale. Remove stems, then chop into rough pieces. Mix together chopped garlic, olive oil, tamari, salt, and pepper; pour over the kale pieces and toss. Add to the roasting chickpeas baking sheet during the final 15 to 20 minutes of roasting. Stir once during roasting.

Arrange all the roasted vegetables on dinner plates and serve with chimichurri sauce (recipe follows).

ⓘ **Tip:** lining baking sheets with parchment paper makes for easy cleanup.

ⓘ **Tip:** use baking sheets with edges to contain any juices from the roasting vegetables.

ⓘ **Information:** garbanzo beans have a delicious nutlike taste and buttery texture. They provide a concentrated source of protein that can be enjoyed year-round and are available either dried or canned.

Avocado Chimichurri Sauce   VG GF DF

1½ T. lemon juice
1½ T. balsamic vinegar
2 T. olive oil
¾ tsp. salt
½ tsp. red chili flakes
¼ tsp. black pepper
½ tsp. oregano
¼ C. chopped fresh parsley
¼ C. chopped fresh cilantro
1 avocado

Mix all ingredients except avocado together. Cut avocado into chunks and mix in, mashing slightly.

Pickled Red Onions VG GF DF   Serves 8

2 large red onions, thinly sliced
1 qt. boiling water
½ C. white wine vinegar
½ C. cold water
½ C. honey
1 tsp. salt
1 tsp. peppercorns
½ tsp. allspice (optional)

Place sliced onions in a bowl; pour boiling water over onions and allow to steep for 5 minutes; drain. Whisk together the vinegar, cold water, honey, salt, peppercorns and allspice. Add the onions and allow to marinate for 10 minutes. Transfer to a jar, cover tightly, and refrigerate until very cold. These pickled onions will keep for several months and get better with age.

Pickled Vegetables VG GF DF

5 C. water
½ lb. carrots, peeled and cut into rounds
½ lb. green beans, trimmed
1 small head cauliflower, broken into florets
2 C. water
1½ C. cider vinegar
¼ C. oil
3 T. brown sugar
1 tsp. salt
1 T. dill weed
6 cloves garlic
¼ C. pickling spice

Bring 5 cups of water to boil in a large pot. Drop in the carrots and parboil for 2 minutes. Remove and plunge into a bowl of ice cold water. Parboil green beans for 3 minutes, move to the cold water. Parboil cauliflower 1 minute, move to cold water. Let all vegetables sit in cold water until cool. Drain and put in a large bowl.

Combine remaining ingredients in a stainless steel saucepan set over medium heat. Bring to a boil and cook for 2 minutes, then pour over the vegetables. Allow to cool to room temperature. Once cooled, put vegetables in screw-top glass jars and fill with as much of the liquid as the jars will hold. Screw on lids and refrigerate for 2 days before using.

Roasted Garlic   VG GF DF

1 or more garlic heads

Heat oven to 350°. Wrap garlic head(s) in a cooking pouch fashioned from aluminum foil. Place in center of oven and roast until garlic is very soft, about 1¼ hours. Remove from oven and cool slightly. Cut garlic heads in half laterally, then using hands, squeeze out the roasted garlic. Use the soft garlic as an appetizer spread or in dishes such as garlic mashed potatoes.

Information: garlic is an excellent source of minerals and vitamins that are essential to good health. The bulbs are one of the richest sources of potassium, iron, calcium, magnesium, manganese, zinc, and selenium.

Homemade Vegetable Stock   VG GF DF   Makes about 20 servings

1 T. olive oil
2 leeks, white and light green portions, chopped
4 medium onions, chopped
6 large carrots, chopped
3 stalks celery, chopped
1 small bunch parsley stems
2 T. fresh marjoram, chopped
2 sprigs fresh thyme
2 bay leaves
1½ gal. cold water

Heat the oil over medium heat in a Dutch oven or large pot. Add vegetables and stir-fry to lightly brown. Add herbs and cold water. Bring to a boil, reduce heat and simmer slightly covered for 1 hour. Strain stock through a fine sieve or cheesecloth-lined colander. Cool and chill or freeze for later use.

Brassicas

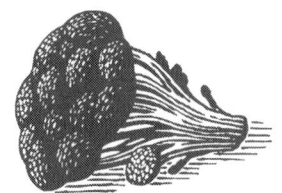

Basic Ways of Cooking & Serving

Vegetable	Preparation	Cooking Time	Ways to Serve
Broccoli	Remove large outer leaves. Make a lengthwise cut in the stem end of each stalk, so broccoli cooks evenly throughout.	Place stalks in pan with about an inch of water, cover, and steam for 8-10 minutes until fork tender.	Buttered with salt and pepper. Vary with fresh herbs, lemon juice, grated cheese, or sauces.
Brussels sprouts	Remove large outer leaves. Make an X cut in the stem end of each sprout to assure even cooking throughout.	Place sprouts in pan with about an inch of water, cover, and steam for 8-10 minutes until fork tender.	Buttered with salt and pepper. Vary with fresh herbs, lemon juice, grated cheese, or sauces.
Cabbage	Remove wilted outside leaves. Shred or cut in wedges. Remove most of the core.	Place in pan with about 1-2 inches of water, cover, and steam wedges 10-15 minutes, shredded 5-8.	Buttered with salt and pepper. Vary with caraway or dill seeds, minced mint, or oregano, vinegar.
Cauliflower	Remove leaves. Leave whole, cutting out center core or cut into florets. Cut off any discoloration.	Place in pan with about 1-2 inches of water, cover, and steam for 20-30 minutes if whole, 8-15 for florets.	Buttered with salt and pepper. Vary with fresh herbs, lemon juice, grated cheese, or sauces.
Kale	Trim off stems thicker than a pencil; cut in 2 inch lengths. Roll kale leaves and chiffonade (cut in narrow strips).	Cook with water to cover. Boil young tender leaves 5-15 minutes; older thicker leaves 20-25. Boil stems 5 minutes before adding leaves. Drain.	Dress with olive oil, butter, lemon juice, or red wine vinegar. Use as an ingredient in other recipes.
Kohlrabi	Remove leaves (cook as greens). Trim off root and stem. Pare; slice, cube or quarter.	Boil 25-40 minutes. Sauté (fry like potatoes) 10-15 minutes.	Buttered with salt and pepper. Vary with fresh herbs.

Now Add Some Creativity!

Broccoli Quiche  Serves 6

1¼ C. fresh broccoli, chopped
3 eggs
¾ C. light cream or milk
⅛ tsp. salt
1½ C. shredded Monterey Jack cheese
1 C. sautéed sliced mushrooms

1 unbaked 9-inch pie crust (recipe follows)
Paprika

Preheat the oven to 350 °. Bring a small pot of water to a boil and cook the broccoli for 5 minutes. Drain the broccoli, plunge it into ice water to stop the cooking process, then drain again well. In a bowl, beat the eggs, cream, and salt. Stir in the broccoli, cheese, and mushrooms. Pour into the pie crust. Sprinkle with paprika. Bake for 50 to 60 minutes, or until a toothpick inserted into the corner comes out clean. Let stand for 10 minutes before serving.

Tip: when cooking fresh brassicas like broccoli, cauliflower or Brussels sprouts, use a steamer insert in your pan, if you have one. This will keep the vegetables out of the cooking water, preserving and keeping nutrients from going down the drain!

Mom's Pie Crust   QE   Makes 2 crusts

2 C. flour
1 t. salt
1/3 C. butter
1/3 C. shortening

Make a paste of 1/4 cup water and 1/3 cup of flour and salt mixture. Cut shortening and butter into flour until it looks like small peas. Mix in the paste until well blended. Divide into 2 disks. Wrap in plastic and refrigerate for 1 hour. This is a never fail dough. You can roll it out multiple times and it will still be flaky. Easy!

Broccoli Florets with Lemon Butter Sauce    Serves 4

2 small shallots or ¼ C. onions, finely chopped
¼ C. white wine
1 lemon, juiced
8 oz. cold, unsalted butter, cut into small pieces
Salt and pepper
1 large head broccoli, broken into florets

Place shallots, wine, and half the lemon juice in a small saucepan, over medium heat. Simmer until almost dry. Reduce heat to very low and stir in a few pieces of the butter, swirling with a whisk until mostly melted. Gradually add remaining butter and whisk constantly until sauce is smooth. Never boil. Season with salt, pepper, and remaining lemon juice to taste. Keep in a warm place, but not over direct heat.

Wash broccoli and steam until crisp tender. Drain broccoli and place in a serving bowl. Serve with lemon butter sauce.

Broccoli Stuffed Potatoes   Serves 6

3 large baking potatoes
3 stalks broccoli
½ tsp. salt
1 T. olive oil
2 T. milk
2 T. grated Parmesan cheese

Preheat oven to 400°. Bake potatoes until soft, about 1 hour. Meanwhile, steam broccoli stalks until crispy tender and bright green, about 5 minutes. Drain, then chop fine. Cut potatoes in half and scoop potato pulp into a bowl. Do not discard the potato shells. Add salt, olive oil, and milk to potatoes and mash. Add the Parmesan cheese and chopped broccoli and mix well. Pile mixture back into the potato shells. Arrange on a baking dish and heat through before serving.

ⓘ**Fact:** broccoli has its roots in Italy, where in ancient Roman times it was developed from wild cabbage, a plant that more resembles collards than broccoli.

Broccoli Gratin QE VG GF   Serves 8

2 bunches broccoli, broken into florets
4 T. unsalted butter, cut into very thin slices
¼ tsp. dried crushed red pepper
Sea salt
Freshly ground black pepper
1/2 - 2/3 C. grated Romano or Parmesan cheese

Cook broccoli in salted water until crisp-tender, but still bright green, about 5 minutes. Drain and cool. Slice florets lengthwise into ¼-inch thick slices. Grease a 9x13 baking dish. Arrange broccoli slices snugly in overlapping rows. Sprinkle with crushed red pepper, sea salt, and black pepper. Distribute the butter slices over the top, then sprinkle with cheese. Bake uncovered in a 425° preheated oven until cheese is melted and broccoli tops are browned, about 20 minutes.

Tip: can be made 8 hours ahead. Cover and chill; increase the baking time a bit, if made ahead and chilled.

Information: broccoli is a nutritional powerhouse, packed with nutrients. It is an excellent source of vitamins C and K, folic acid and fiber; and a good source of manganese, potassium, phosphorus, magnesium, iron, calcium, zinc, B vitamins, vitamin E, omega-3, and protein.

Roasted Brassicas QE VG GF DF   Serves 4

3 lbs. broccoli or cauliflower
Olive oil
Salt and freshly ground black pepper

Clean and break or cut into bite size pieces. You can peel the broccoli stems and cut into pieces. Toss with olive oil, coarse salt and freshly ground black pepper or red pepper flakes. Place on a rimmed baking sheet. Roast at 400° for 10 to 20 minutes until tender and crispy on edges. Broccoli takes longer than cauliflower.

Tip: add color to your meal by using one of the colorful cauliflowers that exist, including green, orange, and purple.

The Best Ever Vegan "Macaroni & Cheese"   VG DF   Serves 6

1 lb. Piccolini pasta (mini bow-tie, mini penne, mini farfalle, etc.)
¼ C. soy-free Earth Balance vegan margarine
1/3 C. flour
2 T. tomato paste
1 T. tahini (paste of ground sesame seeds)
2 T. miso paste
½ C. nutritional yeast flakes
2 C. non-dairy milk such as almond or rice
1 C. broccoli florets, fresh or frozen
1 T. agave (optional)
Sea salt
Black pepper, freshly ground

> *I use gluten-free brown rice pasta and add cayenne & mustard to the sauce. I use less Earth Balance and a bit less almond milk. Broccoli is great, or chop up a head of kale and throw it into the pasta water for the last minute of cooking to blanch.*
> *— Ingrid Lundin*

If using fresh broccoli, steam for 5 minutes and set aside. Cook pasta according to the package directions. In a medium saucepan over medium heat, melt the Earth Balance and whisk in the flour until a thick roux has formed. To the roux add tomato paste, tahini, miso, nutritional yeast, non-dairy milk, and whisk together. Add broccoli and simmer for ten minutes. Generously season with salt and pepper to taste. If a sweeter flavor is desired, add the agave. Toss with the hot pasta and serve. Extra non-dairy milk may be added if a saucier consistency is desired.

ⓘ **Note:** nutritional yeast flakes can be found in the bulk foods aisle of grocery stores or at organic/health foods stores.

Deep Fried Cauliflower   Serves 4 to 5

1 head cauliflower
1 C. pancake mix
1 C. water
1 qt. oil (for frying)

Wash cauliflower and divide into florets. Mix pancake mix and water. Add cauliflower and stir to evenly coat. Heat oil to 350°. Add battered cauliflower and cook until golden brown. Serve with your favorite dipping sauce or dressing.

Cauliflower "Mashed Potatoes"   QE VG GF DF   Serves 4 to 6

2 large heads cauliflower
10 cloves garlic, sliced
Sea salt
2 T. butter or ghee (a type of clarified butter)*
6 T. olive oil
¼ tsp. freshly ground nutmeg
Freshly ground black pepper to taste

Break cauliflower into florets; slice leaves; layer in steamer with garlic; steam until tender. Drain veggies; put them in a food processor, adding oil (and butter if you are using it); add salt and pepper to taste; blend until smooth.

*Omit for vegans

ⓘ **Note:** to make clarified butter, place butter in a saucepan over medium heat. After butter has melted, turn to simmer to allow it to cook. As scum/froth appears on the surface of the butter, spoon it off and dispose of it. Continue this process until all scum has risen and been removed. Allow to cool, then strain/filter to remove any remaining solids. Will keep un-refrigerated for one month, longer if refrigerated.

Brussels Sprouts Salad   QE VG GF DF   Serves 4

3 C. Brussels sprouts, finely shredded
3 C. Swiss chard, stemmed and finely shredded
½ C. golden raisins
½ C toasted nuts
½ C. olive oil
4 T. fresh lemon juice
2 T. maple syrup
1 T. grainy mustard
Salt and black pepper to taste

Shred Brussels sprouts and greens in a food processor. Place in large bowl with nuts and raisins. Place remaining ingredients in a large jar with screw top. Shake until well blended. Pour just enough to lightly coat leaves. Correct the seasoning.

Tangy Mustard Cauliflower QE VG GF   Serves 6 to 8

1 medium head cauliflower
½ C. mayonnaise
Minced onion - ¼ tsp. instant or 2 T. fresh
1 tsp. prepared mustard
½ C. shredded cheddar cheese

Place cauliflower in a 1½-quart casserole. Cover and cook 7 to 8 minutes in the microwave. Combine the mayonnaise, onion, and mustard, mixing well. Place cauliflower on a serving plate, spread top and sides half way down with the mayonnaise mixture. Sprinkle with the cheese, then cook uncovered for one minute in the microwave to heat the topping and melt the cheese.

Many years ago my mother got this recipe from her first microwave cooking class. I never liked cooked cauliflower, but when she made this recipe it made cauliflower so great!
- Sharon Rahm

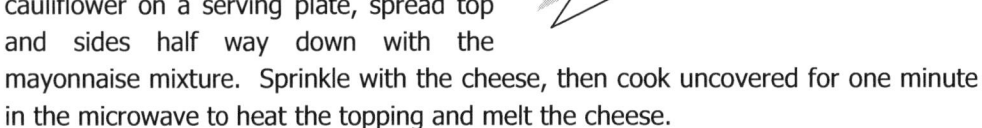

Savory Brussels Sprouts Hash GF DF   Serves 4

2 T. olive oil
2 C. thinly sliced white onions (about 2 medium onions)
Sea salt
1 lb. Brussels sprouts
4 oz. bacon
5 fresh sage leaves, finely chopped
1 medium lemon
Crushed red chili flakes

Heat olive oil in a large skillet set over low heat. Add onions and a pinch of salt. Cook, stirring occasionally, until the onions are caramelized, about 30 minutes. Remove from heat and set aside.

In a large pot, blanch the Brussels sprouts in salted, boiling water until bright green and just tender, about 5 minutes. Remove from the water and set aside to cool a bit. Slice sprouts into shreds.

In medium skillet over medium heat, cook the bacon until crisp, about 5 minutes. Crumble the bacon. Pour off excess bacon fat, leaving about one tablespoon in the pan. Add the shredded Brussels sprouts to the bacon in the pan and cook over medium heat until tender and nicely caramelized, about 5 minutes. Stir in the caramelized onions and sage and heat a bit to bring to serving temperature.

To serve, finish with a few drops of lemon juice, sea salt, chili flakes, and a drizzle of olive oil, all to taste. Serve immediately.

Brussels Sprouts with Caramelized Onions QE VG GF   Serves 8 to 10

1½ lbs. Brussels sprouts, trimmed
6 T. butter
½ lb. thinly sliced onion
Sea salt
Pepper
2 T. apple cider vinegar
4 tsp. sugar
3 T. olive oil
1 C. water

Melt 3 tablespoons butter in a skillet over medium heat. Add onions; sprinkle with sea salt and pepper and sauté until soft and golden in color, about 10 minutes. Add vinegar and sugar. Stir until brown and glazed, about 3 minutes.

Cut sprouts in half lengthwise, then cut each half lengthwise again. In another skillet, heat the oil over medium-high heat. Add sprouts, sprinkle with salt and pepper and sauté until brown at edges, about 6 minutes. Add 1 cup water and the remaining 3 tablespoons butter and sauté until most of the water has evaporated and the sprouts are tender but still bright green, about 3 minutes. Add caramelized onions; season with salt and pepper.

ⓘ**Tip:** Brussels sprouts are often cooked whole. To allow the heat to permeate throughout all of the leaves and better ensure an even texture, cut an "X" in the bottom of the stem before cooking.

ⓘ**Tip:** since cooked Brussels sprouts are small and compact, they make a great snack food that can be simply eaten as is or seasoned with salt and pepper to taste.

ⓘ**Information:** unlike most vegetables, Brussels sprouts are high in protein.

Parmesan Kohlrabi VG GF   Serves 4

2 young kohlrabi bulbs cut into matchsticks
1 large leek
Extra virgin olive oil
1 - 2 T. butter
⅛ tsp. each granulated garlic, black pepper, dried basil
4 oz. Parmesan cheese, finely grated
Kosher salt to taste

Peel kohlrabi. To make matchsticks, turn each bulb into a cube by cutting straight down on one side to stabilize your cuts, then cut straight down, rotate to the opposite side cut straight down. Continue until you have flat surfaces all the way around. Cut into slices, stack, cut down in rows turn the stack cut down again. Match sticks!

Cook or steam kohlrabi until tender, drain, set aside for a minute. Prepare the leek by cutting in half lengthwise. Use only the white and light green bottom of the leek. Rinse well fanning the layers to remove sand. Slice leek into half moon pieces and place in skillet with a small amount of extra virgin olive oil; cook until wilted and almost translucent. Toss in the kohlrabi, then add the butter, Parmesan, and herbs. Salt may be added to taste at the table.

> *Kohlrabi is a misunderstood veggie. Its tender bulbs, before they get big, are sweet and unctuous. Kohlrabi makes a good addition to curry, mashed potatoes or anything with fennel, such as in stuffed trout.*
> *- Virginia Drake Cocayne*

Simple Kohlrabi Salad   Serves 3 to 4

2 kohlrabi, cut into matchsticks
Freshly squeezed lemon juice (1 lemon)
Zest from the lemon
Olive oil
Salt and pepper

Place kohlrabi matchsticks in a bowl. Add the lemon juice, lemon zest, and a few drops of olive oil. Toss to coat, then season to taste with pepper and salt.

Kale with Garlic and Thyme QE VG GF DF   Serves 4

2 lbs. kale, stems and ribs removed
1 T. olive oil
1 medium onion, chopped
1 T. garlic, chopped
Pinch of crushed red pepper flakes
2 tsp. fresh thyme leaves (or ½ tsp. dry)
¼ C. white wine (optional)
Salt and freshly ground black pepper
Grated Parmesan cheese (optional)

Bring a large pot of well-salted water to a rolling boil. Add the kale and cook for 10 minutes, until tender. Drain in a colander, reserving about 1/2 cup cooking liquid. Roughly chop the kale. Heat oil in a large skillet or Dutch oven. Add the onion, garlic, red pepper, and thyme. Cook over medium heat until onions are soft and beginning to turn brown around the edges. Splash in the wine and cook until wine has evaporated. Add the kale and cook 10 minutes more. Season with salt and pepper. Serve sprinkled with grated Parmesan cheese, if desired.

Slathered Kale Slaw QE VG GF DF   Serves 6

6 C. kale, cut in fine ribbons (chiffonade)
Juice of 1 large lemon
1 large ripe avocado
1 tsp. large grain salt
Freshly ground pepper

Place kale ribbons in a bowl and sprinkle with the salt. Pour lemon juice over the kale. Using your hands, massage the salt and lemon juice into the kale. Peel the avocado and cut it into ½-inch pieces. Add two-thirds of the avocado pieces to the kale and massage to release the fats and form a dressing. Once the kale is well-coated, place in a serving bowl and toss with the remaining pieces of avocado. Add pepper to taste.

Kale Salad with Nuts and Dried Fruit   VG GF DF   Serves 4 to 6
(adapted from Bon Appétit, February 2009)

2 T. dried fruit (cranberries, cherries, golden raisins, chopped apricots)
7 T. balsamic vinegar, divided
1 T. rice vinegar
1 T. honey
1 T. extra-virgin olive oil
1 tsp. salt
2 bunches Tuscan kale (about 1 lb.)
2 T. nuts or seeds, lightly toasted

Place dried fruit in small bowl; add 5 tablespoons balsamic vinegar. Let soak overnight. Drain. If you want to make this, but don't have time to soak the fruit, omit that step and increase balsamic vinegar in next step to 3 tablespoons.

Whisk remaining 2 tablespoons balsamic vinegar, rice vinegar, honey, oil, and salt in large bowl. Remove center ribs and stems from kale; thinly slice leaves crosswise. Add kale, dried fruit, and nuts to the vinegar-oil mixture; toss to coat. Let marinate 20 minutes at room temperature, tossing occasionally. Season to taste with salt and pepper.

Kale and Raisin Pasta   Serves 6

½ lb. ground pork (optional)
1 large bunch Lacinato (or curly) kale, cleaned, stemmed, and cut into bite size pieces
½ C. of chopped red or orange bell pepper
¼ C. chopped onion
1 - 2 cloves minced garlic
Smoked hot paprika to taste
Fresh thyme or oregano to taste
Salt and pepper to taste
½ C. or so of golden raisins
2 T. tomato paste
2 T. vermouth
Splash of balsamic or sherry vinegar
1 lb. cooked penne, gemelli, or rigatoni pasta
Grated Romano cheese

> *I prefer DeCecco brand. Just make sure it says "rigate" on the label, or look to see that the pasta has ridges on it.*
> *— Linda Bondurant*

Bring large pot of water to boil. Salt with 1 - 2 tablespoons of coarse salt. Cook pasta to just under al dente. Save 2 cups of pasta water before draining pasta.

Sauté onion and pepper in olive oil. Remove, then brown the pork, if using. Add the aromatics back to pan, with garlic and paprika. Cook for 30 seconds. Add tomato paste and cook another 30 seconds. Add vermouth and deglaze the pan. Add the kale and raisins along with ½ cup or so of the salted pasta cooking water. Cook 3 to 5 minutes and add pasta to pan. Season with vinegar, salt, and pepper to taste. Serve with grated Romano cheese. Also nice with a sprinkle of toasted pine nuts on top.

ⓘTip: kale turns sweeter in cold weather, so it is at its best from mid-fall to early spring. Leave it in the garden during the winter months to extend its use during the time of year when there is little else in the garden.

ⓘTip: store kale in the coldest part of the refrigerator. Keep loosely wrapped, in a plastic bag to keep from wilting.

Kale & Potato Soup VG GF DF   Serves 6 to 8

2 T. olive oil
1 large onion, chopped (or 3-4 leeks, chopped)
2 stalks celery, chopped
3 small carrots, chopped
5 yellow potatoes, chopped
10 C. vegetable stock (see Bulb, Roots & Tubers chapter for homemade recipe)
¾ large bunch of green curly kale, cut into small pieces or ribbons
1 tsp. rosemary or dill (okay to omit if you don't have either of these)
Pepper to taste
1 T. balsamic vinegar

Sauté leeks or onions in olive oil. As they become soft, add celery and carrots. Continue cooking for a few minutes and then add potatoes. Cook for a few minutes more and then add stock, herb of choice, and pepper. Bring to a boil, then reduce heat to medium-low. Cook until potatoes and carrots are soft. Stir in kale and cook for 5 to 7 more minutes (or longer if you like the kale to be well cooked). Turn off heat and add balsamic vinegar and any other optional ingredients that you like. You can make this soup creamy without adding milk, if you take a few cups out, blend it up, and then stir it back into the soup.

> *Kale is my favorite vegetable, and I love Italian Kale the most. I try to eat at least one serving of it every day. It is nutritionally dense, versatile, and delicious, so it's not difficult to work it into your diet on a regular basis. My favorite way to enjoy it is lightly steamed for breakfast as a side to whole-wheat toast with a savory spread. Just tear the kale into pieces, put in on to steam, go do something else for about seven minutes and come back and enjoy!*
>
> *- Erin Majors*

ⓘ **Note:** optional other ingredients, most of which will make this soup no longer vegan, dairy-free, or gluten-free, include garbanzo beans for more protein (add with kale) and milk for a creamy soup (add at the end).

ⓘ **Tip:** to serve, try adding cubed whole wheat bread into each person's soup bowl. Top with shredded Parmesan or Gruyere cheese.

Egg, Kale, and Ricotta on Toast   QE VG   Serves 2

1 large bunch Lacinato kale, stemmed and chopped
Olive oil
2 T. fresh lemon juice
Lemon zest
Salt and pepper to taste
2 large slices hearty bread, toasted
4 T. ricotta cheese
2 eggs

Sauté the kale (water clinging is good) in olive oil until wilted, about 5 minutes. Toss with lemon juice, salt, and pepper. Spread toast with 2 tablespoons ricotta and top each with half of the kale. In olive oil, fry 2 eggs until just set, so yolk is runny. Place egg on each toast, garnish with salt, pepper and lemon zest and eat immediately.

Spoon Salad   QE VG GF   Serves 8

1 large head of kale
½ head of green or red cabbage
1 head of chard
1 bunch watercress
1 bunch parsley
3 large zucchini
3 small beets with greens
3 carrots

Remove ribs from greens. Using the sabatier blade (food processor's multi-purpose "s" blade), process salad ingredients in a food processor. Do like with like, that is, greens all together first, then remove and process beets and carrots together, remove those, and then process zucchini alone. Mix all ingredients well. Serve with chopped avocado and/or chunks of feta with dressing of choice and a sprinkle of seeds (pumpkin, sunflower, sesame, flax). The consistency of the salad, once mixed, is such that you can eat it with a spoon.

ⓘ **Information:** kale is loaded with vitamins A, C, E, and B$_6$; also folate, calcium, manganese, iron and zinc.

Kale, Potato, & Sausage Casserole QE GF   Serves 4

½ - 2/3 bunch of curly-leaved kale, washed and pulled off the stems
3 - 4 russet potatoes, washed, unpeeled and sliced thin
2 - 3 T. butter or lard, plus extra for seasoning
1 lb. bulk Italian sausage (hot or mild depending on desired spice)
1 onion, diced
2 - 3 cloves garlic, minced
1 C. shredded sharp cheddar cheese
Salt and pepper to taste

Preheat oven to 400°. Grease a 9 x 13 inch baking dish and set aside. Wash potatoes, but do not peel them. Arrange potato slices in a single layer in the bottom of the baking dish. Drop a few dots of butter across the top of the potatoes. Add salt and pepper to taste. Bake for about 30 minutes. While the potatoes are baking, brown the sausage in a large skillet. Remove the sausage from the pan to a bowl and set it aside. Sauté the onion until golden and transparent in sausage drippings, add garlic and cook until fragrant. Next add kale and sauté until wilted to about half its original size. Remove from heat. At this point about 30 minutes should have passed. Take the baking dish out of the oven and layer on top of the potatoes the kale, sausage, and cheddar cheese. Return to the oven, uncovered, for 10 minutes.

> *This dish is a huge hit even with kids. I have also made this as a dinner to bring to new mothers or someone who is under the weather. It reheats perfectly.*
>
> *- Kathleen Moore*

Crispy Kale QE VG GF DF   Serves 4 to 6

2 or 3 large bunches of curly or Russian kale
Olive oil
Coarse salt
Red pepper flakes or freshly ground black pepper

Clean and remove stems from kale. Tear or cut into large pieces. Place on oiled rimmed baking sheets. Toss well with olive oil, salt, and pepper. Bake at 400° until crispy, 10 to 20 minutes. Addictive!

Homemade Bibimbap VG GF   Serves 2

2 - 3 T. butter, divided
2 - 3 scallions or ½ onion, chopped
2 cloves garlic, minced
1 inch ginger, minced
2 C. cooked brown rice
2 T. miso (Japanese seasoning)
¼ C. warm water
4 - 5 kale leaves, cut into ribbons (or same amount of chard)
2 eggs

Toppings of your choice: pickled vegetables, avocado, cherry tomatoes, chopped umeboshi plums, soft tofu cubes, seaweed, etc.

Condiments of your choice: kimchi, sauerkraut, Thai chili sauce, tamari, apple cider vinegar, etc.

Heat a large skillet. Place about 2 teaspoons butter, scallions/onion, ginger, and garlic in the skillet. If using chard instead of kale, add it at this time as well. Cook this mixture and when the onions soften, add the cooked rice. While the rice is heating through, dissolve miso in the warm water, then mix into the rice. Stir until heated, then divide between two large bowls.

If using kale in this recipe, melt 2 more teaspoons of butter in the skillet, add the kale and toss until the kale is starting to wilt and glisten. Sprinkle 2 tablespoons of water over the kale, cover and cook until the water is gone and kale is tender. Divide and add to the bowls; sprinkle with a little vinegar, if desired.

Put the remaining butter in the skillet and heat until it sizzles. Break the eggs into the skillet and when the whites are no longer translucent, turn the eggs over and cook to the desired doneness. As the eggs are finishing, re-heat the rice bowls in the microwave. Top each rice bowl with an egg and desired toppings. Add a tablespoon or two of kimchi or sauerkraut and dress with a tiny trail of Thai chili sauce or condiments of your choice. The miso in the rice adds salt, so taste before adding more.

Braised Red Cabbage VG GF DF   Serves 8

1 small head of red cabbage (about 2 lbs.)
1 tsp. salt
Pinch of grated nutmeg
1 T. oil
1 T. red wine vinegar
4 apples, peeled and cut into ¼-inch slices
1 T. brown sugar

Thinly slice (julienne) or shred cabbage. Sprinkle cabbage with salt and nutmeg. Heat oil in Dutch oven; add cabbage and red vinegar. Cover and cook over low heat for at least one hour. Add apples and sugar; cook for another 30 minutes, until cabbage is tender and apples are mostly dissolved.

Sweet-Sour Red Cabbage QE VG GF DF   Serves 6

6 T. cider vinegar
3 T. brown sugar
¾ tsp. caraway seed
¾ tsp. celery seed
6 C. shredded red cabbage
1 - 1½ C. thinly sliced onion
Salt and pepper to taste

Combine the vinegar, brown sugar, caraway seeds, and celery seeds in a small bowl; set aside. Place cabbage and onion in a saucepan; add a small amount of water, cover, and steam until tender, about 15 minutes. Drain. Add vinegar mixture and toss to coat, then season with salt and pepper. Serve warm.

ⓘ**Tip:** late crop cabbage can be stored for 5 to 6 months. Early crop cabbages have a shorter storage time, typically only one month.

ⓘ**Tip:** store the whole head of cabbage in a plastic bag in the refrigerator. The older cabbage gets, the stronger the flavor and odor will be.

ⓘ**Information:** lengthy cooking tends to lower the nutritional value of cabbage.

Bonnie's Cabbage Salad VG GF DF   Serves 4 to 6

1 head cabbage, finely chopped
1 tsp. salt
½ C. green pepper, chopped
½ C. green onions, sliced
1 small carrot, coarsely grated
1 C. apple cider vinegar
½ C. oil
1 - 2 T. sugar
Pepper to taste

> *This is a version of one of those "I've got to have it" recipes. I got the original recipe from my sister, who got it from her friend Bonnie, who got it from her mother.*
> *- Jennifer Grant*

Place chopped cabbage in a bowl and sprinkle with the salt. Let stand for 15 minutes, then squeeze out the water. Add remaining chopped vegetables to the cabbage, then toss with a dressing made by vigorously whisking together the vinegar, oil, sugar and pepper. Refrigerate for one hour before serving.

Jalapeño Slaw VG GF DF   Serves 8

4 C. shredded cabbage
¾ C. grated carrot
½ C. thinly vertically sliced red onion
½ C. chopped fresh cilantro
4 jalapeño peppers, seeded and cut lengthwise in thin slices
1/3 C. freshly squeezed lime juice
1 tsp. sugar
¾ tsp. sea salt
¼ tsp. freshly ground pepper
3 T. olive oil

Place cabbage, carrot, red onion, cilantro and jalapeño peppers in a bowl. Place remaining ingredients in a screw-top jar and shake to blend. Pour over the cabbage mixture and toss well to coat. Cover and chill at least 1 hour.

ⓘ **Information:** raw cabbage contains iron, calcium, potassium, vitamin C, and the B vitamins.

Wasabi Slaw QE VG GF

Serves 4 to 6

2 C. shredded cabbage - green, purple, or savoy
1 grated carrot
2 T. chopped green pepper
2 green onions, sliced
2 T. wasabi powder
1½ T. water
½ C. mayonnaise
1 tsp. freshly grated ginger
1 clove garlic, minced
Salt and pepper
Sesame seeds

Mix the wasabi powder with the water to form a paste. Add a little at a time to the mayonnaise until you reach your desired hotness. Stir in the ginger and garlic. Add salt and freshly ground pepper to taste. Place prepared vegetables in a bowl and add wasabi dressing; to coat. Garnish with a sprinkling of toasted sesame seeds when serving.

ⓘ**Tip:** substitute plain yogurt or sour cream for part or all of the mayonnaise.

ⓘ**Tip:** wasabi powder (made from a variety of green horseradish grown only in Japan) can be found in Asian stores and some supermarkets, as well as on-line.

Koldermer, Lazy Style   Serves 4 to 6

1 lb. ground pork or beef
Olive oil
1 onion, chopped
1 clove garlic, minced
1 T. tomato paste
½ tsp. allspice
1 tsp. paprika
1 small head of cabbage, cored and chopped
2 - 3 T. brown sugar
Salt and black pepper to taste
2 T. vermouth
2 C. cooked rice or bulgur
2 C. chicken broth, to taste
1 T. rice vinegar
1 - 2 C. sour cream or yogurt
Parsley for garnish

> *This is a lazy person's adaptation of the more time-consuming, traditional Swedish Koldermer, which is stuffed cabbage rolls.*
>
> *- Linda Bondurant*

Brown the meat in 2 tablespoons olive oil in a large heavy pot. Remove from pot. Add onions to pot and sauté until limp. Add garlic and cook 30 seconds. Add allspice, paprika, and tomato paste and cook 30 seconds. Deglaze with vermouth.

Add cabbage and cook for 2 minutes, stirring all the time. Add meat, sugar and salt and black pepper to taste. Add rice and broth until stew-like. If dry, add water.

Simmer covered, for 10 minutes until cabbage is tender crisp. Correct seasonings and add vinegar. Mix in parsley and sour cream or yogurt to taste.

ⓘ **Tip:** if you don't have vermouth for de-glazing, simply add vegetable or chicken stock, white wine, clear soda, fruit juice, or plain water. You can be as conservative or creative as you like.

ⓘ **Fact:** in 1984, the Food and Agriculture Organization of the United Nations listed cabbage as one of the top twenty vegetables considered an important food source sustaining the world population.

Rumblededumps ~ Scottish Colcannon VG GF   Serves 4

2 lbs. potatoes, cooked and mashed
3 C. chopped shredded cabbage, steamed until tender
3 - 4 T. butter
½ - 1 C. cream or milk, depending on the dryness of the potatoes
½ C. chopped chives or green onions
Pepper to taste
½ C. grated cheddar cheese

Mix together all the ingredients, except the cheese; place in a buttered baking dish. Top with grated cheese. Bake at 350° until heated through and cheese is melted and beginning to brown.

> *This recipe was inspired by a dish we were served at a B&B in the Highlands of Scotland. The cook, of course, said she didn't use a recipe, but told us the ingredients that were in her Rumblededumps. Once home, we experimented until we came up with these proportions.*
>
> *- Jim Grant*

Veggie Pancakes (Okinomiyaki ~ As You Like It) QE VG GF

2 eggs
1 C. Pamela's flour (gluten-free) or pancake mix of your choice
1 C. shredded cabbage (regular, Savoy, or Chinese)
1 shredded carrot
3 green onions, diced
Water can be added to achieve pancake batter consistency

Prepare vegetables. Beat two eggs and add flour or pancake mix. Add veggies to pancake mix and pour into a large fry pan as you would regular pancakes. Cook on one side until browned, then flip (carefully) and brown other side. Serve with mayonnaise spread on top.

The veggies are pretty interchangeable, so use what your garden has to give - leafy greens, broccoli, chard, shredded zucchini, etc. In Japan, various meats and seafood are included in the pancake. These pancakes work great in the morning, but also make a quick lunch or dinner. They are meant to be savory, not sweet.

ⓘ **Note:** if you use regular flour or a mix of your own, add baking soda.

Summer Vegetable Stir Fry VG GF DF   Serves 2 to 3

4 - 6 baby bok choy, white stems cut into 1-inch pieces, leaves left whole
4 - 5 broccoli florets, sliced lengthwise into ¼-inch thick pieces
1 - 2 C. sugar snap or snow peas, ends trimmed
2 carrots, sliced diagonally into coins
2 - 3 three green onions, sliced
2 T. peanut oil
2 cloves garlic, minced
2 tsp. ginger root, minced
½ C. water or stock
Soy sauce (or other Asian sauce of your choice), to taste
Cooked rice, for serving

In a large skillet, sauté ginger and garlic in oil for about 30 seconds. Remove from the pan and set aside. Add a little more oil to the skillet. Stir-fry the carrots for 1 minute. Add the white pieces of bok choy and broccoli; continue stir-frying for 30 seconds. Add peas and water or stock; cover with a tight-fitting lid and allow to steam until not quite tender, about 2 to 3 minutes. Lift lid and add the bok choy leaves and a little soy sauce. Stir, cover, and let heat through for 30 seconds. Remove lid, add reserved garlic and ginger, and stir-fry until everything is steaming and liquid has nearly evaporated. Adjust seasonings and soy sauce to taste. Serve over rice, sprinkled with the sliced green onions.

ⓘ **Information:** long-grain rice is long and slender. The grains stay separate and fluffy after cooking, so this type of rice is a good choice if you want to serve it as a side dish or as a bed for sauces. The nutlike flavor of Basmati rice makes it a popular long-grain rice.

ⓘ**Tip:** for more protein, add 8 ounces traditional water-packed firm tofu, drained and cut into ½-inch cubes. Add with peas and stock.

ⓘ**Tip:** no bok choy? Cabbage is a good substitute.

ⓘ**Tip:** crispy, sweet bok choy stalks can be eaten raw as a snack or added to salads, sandwiches, and burgers.

Best Sauerkraut Ever! VG GF DF

Ingredients:

25 lbs. kraut cabbage, shredded to yield about 20 lbs. or 10 kg.

200 grams (scant ¾ cup) coarse salt - for 10 kgs of shredded cabbage (ratio is important!)

2 T. whole black peppercorns

5 large carrots, peeled and sliced into rounds

12 bay leaves

6 apples with skin on, washed and pricked several times all over with a fork

Equipment:

- 10-15 gallon food-safe plastic bucket for fermenting the cabbage
- Large new garbage bag(s) or a second bucket or other food-safe container to mix ingredients
- Clean plain cotton kitchen towel to cover cabbage in bucket – preferably white (to guarantee there is no dye to run)
- Clean wooden dowel or wooden spoon with handle long enough to push through the depth of cabbage in the bucket
- Plastic or other sturdy plate that will fit inside the bucket and will cover about ¾ of the bucket opening
- Bricks or other large rock(s), 12-15 lbs in weight, to weigh down the cabbage in the bucket (wrap in lots of plastic to keep cabbage juices from the rock and prevent contamination)
- Ziploc bags or other containers to freeze final product

Day 1 – Make the sauerkraut

Except for the apples, mix all the above ingredients (in one or several batches respecting the ratio of salt to shredded cabbage) in a large bin/doubled up garbage bag/bucket. To make sure the salt and cabbage are well mixed, layer the cabbage and salt in the container. A few minutes after you start mixing the cabbage will start to release its water.

Transfer the mixture to the 10-15 gallon fermentation bucket. Every now and then place an apple between the cabbage layers. Cover the cabbage with a dry clean kitchen towel. Place the plate on top of the towel, followed by the 12 to 15 pounds of weight, making sure that the plate and weight are centered on the cabbage.

Place the bucket in a warm room, 65 to 70° F. It will stay in this location until it is ready.

Day 5

Remove weights, plate, and towel from the bucket, placing them somewhere clean so they will not get dirty – you are not done with them yet. Push a clean long stick through the cabbage 6 to 8 times to allow the fermentation gases to rise.

If the cabbage begins to go moldy on top, remove the moldy portion and add about 4 cups of water - there is not enough moisture in the cabbage. Replace the towel, plate, and only 5 pounds of the weight back on the cabbage. If there is juice on the surface that is just fine – do not remove it.

Day 6

Repeat Day 5 process - remove weights, plate, and towel from the bucket, placing them somewhere clean so they will not get dirty – you are not done with them yet. Push a clean long stick through the cabbage 6-8 times to allow the fermentation gases to rise.

Replace the towel, plate, and only 5 pounds of the weight back on the cabbage.

If there is juice on the surface that is just fine – do not remove it.

Day 8 to 10

On day 8, check if cabbage is ready: it should be soft but still a little crunchy when you bite through it. If it is not ready, give it a few more days until it reaches the soft but crunchy stage; the total time may depend on how warm it is where you are letting it ferment. Keep the towel, plate, and 5 pounds of weight on the cabbage until it is done.

When cabbage is ready, remove from bucket and pack in Ziploc bags or other containers. Discard apples. If the cabbage is very wet squeeze out some of the moisture. When packed there should be a little juice accumulation in the corners of the Ziploc bag. Freeze.

The cabbage will last frozen for a year, maybe longer, as long as it doesn't get freezer burn.

Cooking with the kraut, the Russian way!

Thaw about 2 pounds of the sauerkraut. If the cabbage is very wet, squeeze some of the juices into a bowl – do not throw the juice away yet.

Chop one medium onion and about 5 slices of bacon (or sausage, ham, etc… as long as there is a reasonable amount of fat that will be rendered when cooking). Fry in a large pan until onion is golden brown and bacon is soft and brown. Add some black pepper.

Add the cabbage, mix, and cook slowly for at least one hour, up to 2 preferably. Make sure you have 1 to 2 bay leaves in with the cabbage. Stir occasionally to make sure it does not stick and burn to your pan – keep covered while cooking. If the cabbage is getting too dry and sticking to the pan, add some of the retained juice, or water. When done remove bay leaves, and it is ready to eat.

> *When I was a young child in Montana, I helped my grandmother in her garden. She had over an acre in food production -- enough to feed my grandparents, my family of four and my aunt and uncle's family of three with enough left over for friends and relatives. My favorites? New potatoes, shell peas, and onions in cream sauce, fresh Italian flat green beans, carrots, and sauerkraut. This sauerkraut recipe, honed to perfection by a friend, eclipses my grandmother's. In my family, "You're a good cook, Doris" means we've met my now deceased grandmother.*
>
> *- Liza Rognas*

Corn, Peas, Beans & Pods

Basic Ways of Cooking & Serving

Vegetable	Preparation	Cooking Time	Ways to Serve
Corn	Remove husks, silk and blemishes just before cooking.	Boil in unsalted water to cover for 5-8 minutes. Salt toughens corn.	On cob with butter, salt and pepper. Vary with minced cilantro or chili powder. Cut from the cob, served in butter or cream.
Green Beans	Snap off ends. Leave whole and slice into thin strips lengthwise for French-style or crosswise into 1 inch lengths. If desired, add a clove of garlic or a bit of onion while cooking.	Boil whole 15-20 minutes; cross cut 15-20 minutes; French cut 10 minutes.	Buttered with salt and pepper. Vary by tossing with bacon drippings. Vary with fresh herbs - basil, marjoram, dill weed, savory, or thyme.
Lima Beans	Snap pods open and remove beans.	Boil 20-30 minutes.	Buttered with salt and pepper. Vary with savory or sage. Or serve in cream.
Peas Shelled	Shell just before cooking. Add 1 tsp. sugar and a few pods to the water for additional flavor.	Boil 8-15 minutes.	Buttered with salt and pepper. Vary with basic, mint, savory, thyme, or tarragon. Vary by serving creamed.
Pea Pods	Snap off tips and ends; peel strings from both sides.	Cook in 1 inch water or use steamer basket. Depending on desired crispness, cook in a covered pan for 1-5 minutes, May also be sautéed in a small amount of cooking oil.	Season with salt and pepper if desired. Vary with fresh herbs - mint, basil, thyme, tarragon.

ⓘTip: this group of vegetables is best eaten as soon after picking as possible; eat before the natural sugars can turn to starch, making the vegetable tough and less flavorful.

ⓘTip: more beans than you can use fresh? Try drying them for use in soups during the winter months. Let whatever varieties you are growing develop seeds and dry while still on the vine. Read how to do it in the Legumes and Grains chapter.

ⓘTip: all parts of the pea plant are edible. As the leaves and stems mature, they tend to get tough, but when young, pea shoots are tender and tasty. Pea tendrils are wonderful as edible garnishes and snacks; and they make a great addition to soups, salads, and stir-fries.

Now Add Some Creativity!

Grilled Corn in the Husks   VG GF   Serves 8

8 large ears fresh corn in the husks
¾ C. unsalted butter, room temperature
2 tsp. chili powder
1 tsp. salt
1 tsp. ground cumin
¼ tsp. black pepper

Mix butter and seasonings in a small bowl. Pull back the husks from the corn, leaving husk attached, but removing the corn silk. Using a small spatula, spread the seasoned butter generously over each ear. Pull the husks back into place, enclosing the corn and tie with kitchen string in two places to secure. Submerge prepared ears of corn in a large pot of cold water. Soak at least 15 minutes and up to an hour. Heat barbecue to medium-high heat. Drain the corn and grill on the barbecue until cooked through and slightly charred, about 15 minutes. Be sure to turn occasionally. Cut strings, arrange on a platter, and serve.

ⓘ **Tip:** seasonings may be adjusted based on your taste preferences. Experiment with flavors by using different herbs and spices; can be prepared (up to the point of soaking) one day ahead. Cover and refrigerate.

Summer Succotash Salad   QE VG GF DF   Serves 8

8 ears sweet corn, shucked
½ C. diced green or red pepper
2 (16-oz.) cans pinto or red kidney beans, drained and rinsed
¼ C. rice vinegar
¼ C. olive oil
¼ C. chopped chives
Salt and pepper to taste

Shave corn kernels from the cob. Cook in boiling, salted water for 1 minute. Toss with remaining ingredients and serve.

Corn and Potato Chowder VG GF   Serves 12

8 ears sweet corn, shucked
1 T. olive oil
2 large onions, chopped
2 stalks celery, chopped
1 lb. new potatoes, cut into 1-inch chunks
3 sprigs fresh thyme (or 1 tsp. dried thyme leaves)
1 bay leaf
3 tsp. salt
1 stick (4 oz.) unsalted butter
3 qts. vegetable stock (see Bulb, Roots & Tubers chapter for recipe)
4 tsp. cornstarch, dissolved in ¼ C. cold water
1 qt. cream or milk
Salt and pepper to taste
2 T. fresh chives, chopped

Cut corn from cobs and set kernels aside. Do not throw cobs away! Heat olive oil in a large soup pot on medium-high heat. Add corn cobs, corn kernels, onions, celery, potatoes, thyme, bay leaf, and salt to pot and cook until onions are translucent, about 5 minutes. Add butter and cook gently, allowing vegetables to stew in the butter for about 5 more minutes. Add vegetable stock. Raise heat and bring to a boil. Lower heat to a simmer and cook for 10 minutes more. Remove corn cobs. Stir in cream (or milk), and adjust seasoning with salt and pepper to taste. Serve in soup bowls with a sprinkling of chives on top.

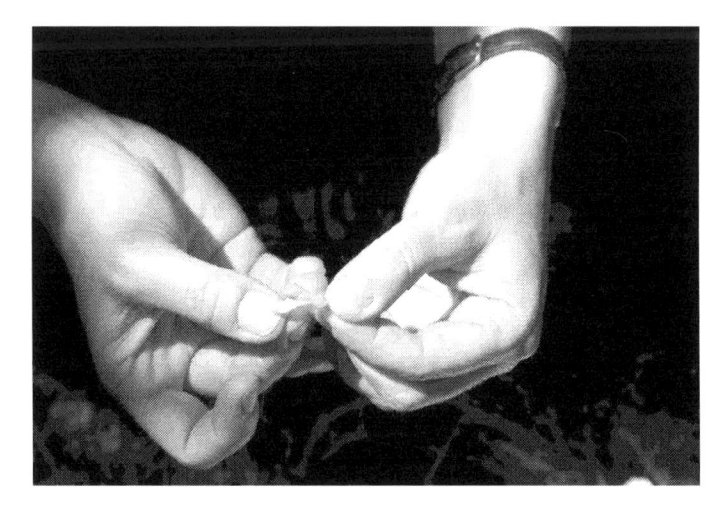

Corn Pudding VG GF   Serves 12

8 T. unsalted butter, melted
3 C. fresh corn kernels (about 4-5 ears)
2 eggs
1 C. sour cream
9 oz. Monterey Jack or Pepper Jack cheese, cut into ½-inch cubes
½ C. cornmeal
1 - 2 jalapeño peppers, finely chopped or 1 (4-oz.) can green diced chilies, drained and patted dry
½ tsp. salt
½ C. grated Parmesan cheese

Preheat oven to 350°. Grease a 2-qt. casserole dish. Purée one cup of the corn kernels with the melted butter and eggs in a blender or food processor. Place all remaining ingredients, except the Parmesan cheese, in a large bowl. Add puréed corn and mix well. Pour into casserole dish, sprinkle with Parmesan, and bake until puffed and golden, about 30 minutes. If pudding looks puffed, but the top is not brown, place under broiler for a couple of minutes until golden spots appear. Watch closely so the pudding top doesn't burn.

Tip: for more bite, add a dash or two of Tabasco or other hot sauce to the corn mixture before pouring it into the casserole dish.

Tip: to make this delicious vegetable side dish in winter, use frozen corn in place of the fresh kernels.

Fact: the traditional name for corn is maize, by which it was known to the Native Americans and many other cultures throughout the world.

Fact: although we most often think of corn as being yellow in color, it can be found in an array of colors, including red, pink, black, purple, and blue.

Information: corn contains B vitamins, as well as vitamins A and C, folate, phosphorus, manganese, and several antioxidants.

Tip: to store corn, leave the corn in the husk and refrigerate as soon as possible. If husked, place in a plastic bag and refrigerate. It is best to eat corn as soon as possible.

Jalapeño Corn Cakes QE VG   Serves 6

1 large egg
1 C. milk
¾ C. corn meal, preferably stone-ground
½ C. flour
½ tsp. sea salt
2 tsp. baking powder
1 tsp. fresh chopped marjoram leaves
3 green onions, sliced (set some of the green pieces aside)
1 jalapeño pepper, seeded and chopped
2 C. fresh corn kernels
¼ C. vegetable oil
Sour cream or plain yogurt

Whisk the egg and milk together in a medium bowl. Add cornmeal, flour, salt, baking powder, and marjoram, stirring to combine. Fold in the onions, jalapeño, and corn. Heat 2 tablespoons oil in a large skillet over medium heat. Scoop ¼-cup portions of the corn batter into the skillet. Cook, turning once, until puffed and browned, about 6 minutes total. Repeat with remaining batter, adding more oil between batches. Serve with sour cream/yogurt and the reserved green onion slices.

Pea Pods in Orange Sauce QE VG GF   Serves 4

3 C. snow peas, steamed until crisp-tender
2 tsp. water
2 tsp. frozen orange juice concentrate
1 tsp. butter
¼ tsp. sesame seeds

Combine all ingredients, except the pea pods, in a small saucepan. Cook and stir over low heat until butter melts. Toss pea pods with the orange butter and serve.

ⓘ**Tip:** try substituting other cooked vegetables such as broccoli, Brussels sprouts, or carrots.

ⓘ**Information:** pea pods are a good source of vitamins A, C and K; also iron.

Pea Pod Salad with Ginger Dressing QE VG GF DF   Serves 4

½ lb. edible pod peas
3 qts. bite-size pieces of butter lettuce
2 kiwi, peeled and thinly sliced
1 orange, sectioned and cut into pieces
1 tsp. finely shredded orange peel
¾ C. orange juice
2 T. red wine vinegar
2 T. minced crystallized ginger or 1 tsp. grated fresh ginger

Cook pea pods in water until tender-crisp, about 2 minutes. Immerse in cold water immediately to stop cooking. Let cool for awhile in the cold water, then drain. Meanwhile, place the orange peel, orange juice, vinegar, and ginger in a screw-top jar and shake vigorously until blended. Mix the lettuce, pea pods, kiwi slices, and orange pierces, then equally divide between four salad plates. Spoon the dressing over each and serve.

Tip: dressing may be made a day ahead. Cover and chill until ready to make the salad.

Citrusy Pea Pod Salad QE VG GF DF   Serves 4

2 C. snow pea pods (snap peas will also do)
1 orange, sectioned and cut into pieces
3 green onions, sliced
4 C. baby spinach
2 T. finely chopped fresh mint

Blanch peas in boiling water for 1 minutes or until they turn a brilliant green. Drain and rinse immediately in cold water. Pat pea pods dry with a paper towel, then put them into a large bowl. Add the remaining ingredients and toss. Drizzle with citrus vinaigrette (recipe follows) and serve immediately.

Citrus Vinaigrette

In a jar with a screw top lid, shake until blended the juice of one lemon and one orange, one teaspoon honey, and four tablespoons olive oil.

Snow Pea Stir-Fry QE VG GF DF   Serves 4

2 C. fresh snow peas, cut into strips
1 C. carrots, cut into thin strips
1 C. mushrooms, sliced
2 green onions, thinly sliced
Cooking oil
Soy sauce to taste

Lightly coat a skillet or wok with cooking oil. Add snow peas, carrots, mushrooms, and onions. Stir-fry over medium heat until vegetables are tender-crisp. Add soy sauce to taste, if desired. Serve as a side dish or over cooked rice or pasta.

Minted Sweet Peas QE VG GF   Serves 4

2 C. shelled fresh peas (about 2 lbs. pods)
½ tsp. sugar
2 T. butter
Salt and pepper to taste
3 T. fresh mint leaves, chopped

Simmer peas and sugar until bright green and tender, about 5 minutes. Drain, then toss with butter, salt, pepper, and mint.

Tip: vary this recipe by adding an equal amount of edamame as peas. Purée after simmering step and before incorporating the other ingredients.

Roasted Snap Peas QE VG GF DF   Serves 6

1 lb. sugar snap peas
1 T. olive oil
Sea salt
2 T. chopped fresh chives

Preheat broiler. Line a large baking sheet with foil. Toss peas with oil and spread in a single layer on the baking sheet. Broil about 2 minutes until crisp-tender and beginning to brown in spots, stirring once. Transfer to serving bowl; sprinkle with sea salt and chives; serve.

Quick and Easy Snow Pea Salad   QE VG GF DF   Serves 6

½ lb. snow peas, trimmed and strings removed
½ lb. fresh mushrooms, stems removed, thinly sliced
1 large red bell pepper, cut into thin strips
4 T. olive oil
2 T. rice wine vinegar (any flavor vinegar will do)
Dash of soy sauce

Blanch snow peas in boiling water until they turn bright green, about 1 minute, then plunge into cold water to stop cooking process. Drain well, place on paper towels and pat dry. Cut pods in half and place in salad bowl. Add the sliced mushrooms and pepper strips. Whisk together the remaining ingredients and pour over the salad vegetables. Toss and serve.

Pea Spaetzle (German egg noodles)   VG   Serves 8

3½ C. fresh peas, removed from pods and steamed until cooked through
4 eggs
1 C. chicken broth
2 T. + 4 T. chopped fresh chives
2 T. chopped mint
1/3 C. mint small leaves
2½ tsp. coarse salt
2 C. flour
6 T. butter
¼ tsp. ground nutmeg
1 C. cherry or grape tomatoes, cut in halves or quarters

Combine 2 cups of the peas, eggs, 1/2 cup of the broth, 2 tablespoons of the chives, the chopped mint, and salt in a blender. Purée until smooth. Pour into a large bowl, then stir in flour. Bring a large pot of salted water to a boil. Working with 1/3 cup batter at a time and using a rubber scrapper, press the spaetzle batter through a colander (or some other implement) that has ¼-inch holes. Boil each batch 3 minutes. Using a slotted spoon, remove the spaetzle to another colander or large sieve to drain, then place in a large bowl. Toss with 2 tablespoons butter. The spaetzle and remaining peas can be covered and refrigerated for a day at this time, otherwise proceed with the preparation as follow: melt 4 tablespoons butter in large skillet; add spaetzle, remaining 1/2 cup of broth and simmer until the broth is almost evaporated and spaetzle heated through. Stir frequently, about 5 minutes. Add remaining peas, remaining chives, mint leaves, nutmeg, and tomatoes. Toss until heated through. Season with salt and pepper.

Herbed Green Beans VG GF DF   Serves 4

4 T. olive oil
4 T. fresh lemon juice
1 tsp. Dijon mustard
2 cloves garlic, minced
½ tsp. sea salt
1 lb. green beans, ends trimmed, julienned
¼ C. chopped red onion
¼ C. chopped fresh herbs of your choice (marjoram, dill, basil, parsley, or a mix)
1 tsp. grated lemon peel

Whisk together oil, mustard, garlic, and sea salt; set aside. Cook beans in boiling salted water until crisp-tender, about 3 minutes. Run under cold water to stop cooking. Combine all ingredients with the dressing, toss, then refrigerate at least 2 hours or overnight.

Tip: substitute yellow string beans for half of the green beans to make this side dish more colorful.

Oven-roasted Green Beans QE VG GF DF   Serves 4

1 lb. fresh green beans
1½ T. olive oil
¾ tsp. sea salt
½ tsp. freshly ground black pepper

Preheat oven to 425°. Trim the ends from the green beans. Put beans in a bowl and toss with the remaining ingredients. Spread in a single layer on a baking sheet. Roast, turning half way through, until lightly caramelized and crisp tender, about 12 to 15 minutes.

Dilly Beans VG GF DF   Makes about 3 quarts

2/3 C. coarse sea salt
2 lbs. small, tender green or yellow beans, ends trimmed
6 fresh dill sprigs
6 small garlic cloves, smashed
3 small dried red chilies (such as cayenne)
1 T. dill seeds
1 tsp. black peppercorns, crushed

Stir salt into 1 gallon warm water in a large bowl, stirring until salt is dissolved. Let cool to room temperature. Layer beans with remaining ingredients in a large ceramic, glass or stainless steel bowl. Add salt brine to cover. Put remaining brine in a sturdy re-sealable plastic bag and set on top of beans to keep them submerged. Cover bowl with a clean kitchen cloth and let stand at room temperature until bubbles form around the edge of the bowl, about 4 to 5 days. Spoon off any foam from surface of the brine. Continue to let stand at room temperature, discarding foam as necessary, until beans are pickled, about 2 weeks. Using a slotted spoon, divide beans and herbs between 3 clean 1 qt. jars. Set strainer with two layers of cheesecloth over a large pitcher and pour brine through the strainer. Pour over beans in jars, leaving ½-inch space on top. Cover; chill up to 2 months. Use as a snack or in recipes such as the following Dilly Bean Potato Salad.

Dilly Bean Potato Salad QE VG GF   Serves 6 to 8

1 C. thinly sliced green onions
6 T. red wine vinegar
3 lbs. baby yellow potatoes
Freshly ground pepper
½ C. mayonnaise
½ C. unflavored yogurt or light/non-fat sour cream
⅛ tsp. paprika
3 C. trimmed watercress or arugula
1 C. dilled green beans, cut into 2-inch pieces
2 - 3 hard-cooked eggs, peeled and quartered
¾ C. flat-leaf parsley or celery leaves, coarsely chopped

Combine green onions, vinegar, and a pinch of salt in a small bowl. Set aside. Cook potatoes in salted boiling water until just tender, about 30 minutes. Drain and transfer to a large bowl. Lightly crush potatoes with the back of a large spoon. Add vinegar mixture to hot potatoes and toss to incorporate. Season with salt and pepper. Whisk together mayonnaise, yogurt, and paprika, then add to potatoes and toss to combine. Fold in watercress, beans, and eggs and season to taste with salt, pepper, and vinegar, if desired. Garnish with chopped parsley. Chill if not serving immediately. Return to room temperature and stir in more mayonnaise-yogurt mixture if dry.

Dilly Beans in a Hurry   VG GF DF

½ lb. green beans, tops removed
¼ C. fresh dill, chopped
1 C. white wine vinegar
1 C. water
2 tsp. sugar
2 tsp. salt
2 tsp. pickling spice
1 clove garlic, peeled

Place green beans and dill in a bowl. Combine remaining ingredients in a saucepan. Bring to a boil and cook until sugar and salt dissolve, about 1 minute. Pour over beans and dill. Let stand for two hours. Drain to serve. To store, pack in a glass jar or other airtight container and refrigerate. Will keep up to a week in the refrigerator.

Marinated Green Bean & Potato Salad QE GF DF   Serves 6

¾ lb. green beans, trimmed
½ lb. yellow (wax) beans, trimmed
½ lb. fingerling potatoes, cut in half lengthwise
4 T. white wine vinegar
1 T. olive oil
½ tsp. sea salt
½ tsp. ground pepper
1 T. minced fresh parsley
2 bacon slices, cooked and crumbled

Cook green and yellow beans in boiling water until crisp-tender, about 5 minutes. Drain, then plunge into cold water to stop cooking; drain again. Place potatoes in a pan, covered with water; bring to a boil. Reduce heat and simmer until tender, about 5 minutes. Drain, then return potatoes to the pan. Add 2 tablespoons vinegar to the pan; place over medium heat and bring to a boil, then remove from heat. In a small bowl, whisk together the remaining 2 tablespoons vinegar, the oil, and ¼ teaspoon each of the salt and pepper. Drizzle the beans with the vinegar mixture; toss to coat. Arrange the beans on a serving platter; top with the potatoes, followed by the remaining salt, pepper, parsley, and bacon. Serve at room temperature.

Schnittbohnensalat ~ German Green Bean Salad VG GF DF   Serves 4

1 lb. fresh green beans
¼ C. stock (water from cooking the green beans)
3 T. vinegar
3 T. vegetable oil
2 medium onions, thinly sliced
½ tsp. dry dill seed
1 tsp. sugar

Slice green beans lengthwise (French cut) Cook beans in boiling salted water until just tender; reserve ¼ cup cooking liquid and drain off the rest. Prepare sauce by combining the vinegar, oil, reserved vegetable stock, onions, dill seed, and sugar; stir until blended. Pour mixture over beans; marinate several hours before serving.

Pesto Pasta with Green Beans & Potatoes QE VG   Serves 4 to 6

1 - 2 new potatoes, peeled and cut into cubes no larger than ¾-inch
½ lb. fresh green beans, trimmed and cut into 2-inch pieces
12 oz. dried linguini, fettuccini or penne pasta
¾ C. pesto (see recipe in Herbs chapter or use store-bought)
Salt and pepper
Grated Parmesan cheese
Fresh basil leaves

This is a recipe inspired by a pasta dish served at an Italian restaurant we used to frequent when in Ashland, Oregon for the Oregon Shakespeare Festival. The restaurant is no longer there, so I had to come up with my own version of this decadent dish.
- Jennifer Grant

Bring 3 quarts water to a boil in a large pot over high heat. Add potatoes and pasta and cook uncovered for 8 minutes. Add the beans and cook, stirring occasionally, until potatoes are tender and pasta and beans tender but not soft, about 4 or 5 minutes longer. Drain, reserving 1 cup cooking liquid. Return pasta mixture to the pan and add pesto and ¾ cup cooking liquid. Mix gently, adding more cooking liquid if pasta mixture seems dry. Add salt, pepper and Parmesan cheese to taste, tossing lightly. Serve in pasta bowls, garnished with a sprinkling of additional Parmesan and a few fresh basil leaves.

Lima Beans with Pancetta QE GF DF   Serves 4

1 lb. frozen lima beans or shelled edamame
2 T. minced shallots
3 T. chopped pancetta or bacon
Balsamic vinegar, red pepper flakes and salt to taste

Fry pancetta until crisp. Remove from pan. Add beans and shallots and sauté until done, about 5 minutes. Add bacon, red pepper flakes, salt and balsamic vinegar to taste. Sherry vinegar works well, also.

ⓘ**Fact:** also known as chad beans, lima beans originated in Peru or Guatemala.

Mustardy Green & Yellow Beans QE VG GF DF   Serves 4 to 6

½ lb. each green and yellow wax beans
1 T. olive oil
2 T. Dijon mustard
1 T. honey
Juice from ½ lemon
1 T. finely minced fresh parsley
Salt and freshly ground pepper to taste

Bring a pan of water to a boil over high heat, add beans and cook for 2 to 3 minutes. Drain, reserving 1-2 tablespoons of the cooking water. Rinse in cold water to stop the beans from further cooking. Transfer to serving dish and set aside. Place the remaining ingredients in a screw top jar and shake to blend. Add some of the reserved cooking water, if needed, to thin the dressing a bit. Pour over the beans, toss to coat and serve.

Vegetable & Barley Soup VG DF   Serves 6 to 8

1 C. pearl barley
8 C. vegetable stock (see Bulb, Roots & Tubers chapter for recipe)
4 large tomatoes (preferably Roma, but any type will work)
3 - 4 carrots, peeled and quartered
10 oz. fresh mushrooms, thickly sliced
1 large onion, cut in chunks
1 bell pepper, cut in chunks
1 - 2 medium zucchini, cut in thick slices
3 cloves unpeeled garlic
2 T. olive oil
Fresh thyme sprigs
1 - 2 bay leaves
Fresh chopped parsley

Preheat oven to 400°. Grease a rimmed baking sheet and arrange tomatoes, carrots, mushrooms, onion bell pepper, zucchini, and garlic on sheet. Drizzle with oil; sprinkle with salt and pepper. Roast until vegetables are tender and brown around the edges, stirring occasionally, about an hour.

Peel garlic and set aside. Coarsely chop half the roasted vegetables and set aside. Transfer garlic and remaining vegetables from the sheet to a large pot. Add 1/2 cup vegetable stock to baking sheet and scrape up the browned bits; add to pot. Add remaining broth, barley, thyme, and bay leaf to the pot. Bring to a boil, reduce to simmer and cook covered until barley is tender, 45 to 60 minutes. To serve, sprinkle with fresh chopped parsley.

Tip: to reduce final cooking time by more than half, soak barley overnight (two cups water for each cup barley). Drain before adding to soup mixture.

Tip: selecting mushrooms ~ for a light, delicate mushroom flavor, look for a closed veil (the area under the mushroom cap); for a richer, more developed flavor, look for an open veil. Store mushrooms in a paper bag and always refrigerate. No need to clean mushrooms until ready to use. Gently wipe surface with a damp cloth to remove any particles; never soak.

Summer Vegetable Pot Pie VG   Serves 6 to 8

5 C. fresh garden vegetables (cooked sliced green beans, cooked shelled peas, cooked corn kernels, sliced zucchini, diced carrots, chopped green pepper, chopped onion, etc.)
5 T. butter (divided into 2 T. and 3 T.)
4 T. flour 1 tsp. salt
1/3 tsp. freshly ground pepper
¼ tsp. nutmeg
¼ tsp. garlic powder
2½ C. vegetable (or chicken broth for non-vegetarian version)

In a skillet, melt 2 tablespoons butter. Sauté any onion, carrots, and green pepper being used. Place this mixture in a casserole, along with the other prepared vegetables. Make a white sauce out of remaining 3 tablespoons butter, flour, salt, pepper, nutmeg, and broth. When thickened, pour over the contents of the casserole. Top with herbed or cheese biscuits (recipe follows), sprinkle with paprika and bake in a 425° oven for about 25 minutes.

Tip: for a heartier pie, add cooked chicken pieces to the mix.

Pot Pie Biscuits QE   Makes about ten 1¾-inch biscuits

1 C. flour
1½ tsp. baking powder
½ tsp. salt
3 T. shortening
1/3 C. milk
1 T. fresh herbs, minced (rosemary, sage, marjoram, thyme, etc.) or
½ C. shredded cheddar cheese.

Measure and mix dry ingredients in a bowl. Cut in shortening with a pastry blender until mixture looks like "meal." Stir in the minced herbs or cheese and almost all of the milk. Too much milk makes biscuits sticky, not enough makes biscuits dry. Add remaining milk if dough is too dry. Empty dough onto a floured cloth or board and knead lightly for about 30 seconds. Roll out to about ½-inch thickness and cut with a biscuit cutter. Arrange biscuits on top of the pot pie ingredients and bake as directed in recipe on previous page (Summer Vegetable Pot Pie).

Legumes & Grains

Basic Ways of Cooking & Serving

Vegetable	Preparation	Cooking Time	Ways to Serve
Dried Beans, such as black bean, cannellini, garbanzo, cranberry, navy, kidney, pinto and lima	Use straight out of the can, usually rinsed and drained. For dry beans, soak overnight and cook in liquid until desired tenderness is reached - time will vary with bean type. May also be cooked in a pressure cooker or in a slow-cooker.	Stove top 1½ - 3 hours. Pressure Cooker - 11-18 minutes. Slow Cooker - 1½ hours on High; 6-8 hours on Low. Actual time depends on variety of bean.	Classic for soup and chili. Also baked bean dishes, salads and side dishes. Often used in Mexican, Cuban, South American, Southwestern, Tuscan, Middle East, Portuguese, and Spanish recipes.
Dried Peas, such as green split and yellow split	Pre-soak for 6-7 hours. Cook in liquid.	30 to 40 minutes, if presoaked; much longer if not presoaked.	Classic for soup, but too mushy when cooked for salads. Often used in Middle Eastern, African, and Indian recipes.
Lentils, such as red, green and brown	Pre-soaking not required. Cook separately in liquid. May be stirred into a dish such as risotto, depending on the variety of lentil.	20 to 45 minutes, depending on variety	Good substitute for split peas in soups. Also in lentil soups and salads, and as an ingredient in such dishes as croquettes, risottos, and veggie burgers. Often used in Middle Eastern, Spanish, French, and Indian recipes.
Grains	It is advisable to rinse whole grains before cooking in order to clean the grain and remove any debris that may be present.	Some grains are best if soaked before cooking; cooking time is greatly reduced. It is also often beneficial to toast grains before cooking. This gives the grain a head start on the cooking process, and often reduces the required cooking time when the grain is boiled, steamed, or baked after toasting. Quick toasting, on the stovetop or in the oven, adds flavor to the final dish.	Grains can be used as ingredients in a variety of dishes and recipes, such as in soups, casseroles, salads, breads, pancakes, and meatloaf.
Barley	Pearl barley needs no pre-soaking. Cook in twice the amount of liquid as the barley measure.	30 to 45 minutes or 10-12 minutes for "quick" barley.	Classic for soup. Also used in stews, salads, risottos, pilafs, casseroles, side dishes, and veggie burgers.
Bulgur	Simply needs to be soaked in water that has been brought to a boil and is then poured into a pan or dish containing the bulgur. Use 2½ cups boiling water for 1 cup bulgur.	Cover pan of bulgur and allow to stand for 30 minutes. Drain and fluff. Ready to use.	Use in salads, pilaf, veggie burgers and side dishes. Use place of rice or pasta. Often used in Middle Eastern and Asian recipes.

Chart continues on the next page.

Polenta	Cooked in liquid: 4 parts liquid to 1 part polenta.	25 to 30 minutes	Classic side dish. Also used as a base for ragouts, chili, and similar dishes.
Oats	Cooked in liquid or used dry as an ingredient.	1 to 30 minutes; time varies when cooking, based on variety of oats being used, i.e., old-fashioned, quick, steel-cut.	Classic breakfast food. Also used as ingredient in muffins, cookies, granola, cereal bars, crumbles, breads, meatloaf.
Quinoa	Cook in liquid, like rice. Two parts liquid to 1 part quinoa. May be cooked in a rice cooker, in the same way you would do white rice.	12 to 15 minutes	Use in place of rice or pasta. Used in side dishes, salads, pilafs, croquettes, stuffed peppers, veggie burgers, breads.
Teff Grain	Cook covered until liquid is absorbed. Two cups water to 1/2 cup teff.	15 to 20 minutes. Let stand uncovered for 5 minutes.	Grain - Serve as a porridge, "polenta" and in veggie burgers, muffins, pancakes. Flour - Use in place of wheat and other flours in recipes for bread, cookies, pie crust, muffins, etc.
Amaranth	Cook in liquid, 1½ cups water to ½ cup amaranth	Simmer for 25 minutes or until all water is absorbed.	Grain - porridge, pilafs, side dishes, puffed or popped (like popcorn). Also as an ingredient in soups or stews and seed ingredient and topping for breads. Flour - Use in place of wheat and other flours in recipes for bread, cookies, pancakes, muffins, etc.

Tip: one cup dried beans, peas or lentils typically yields 2¼ to 2½ cups cooked.

Tip: one cup pearl barley yields 3½ to 4 cups cooked;

Tip: one cup bulgur yields 2½ to 3 cups cooked.

Tip: polenta is available in different forms - coarse ground polenta, finely ground polenta, instant polenta, white polenta, and precooked (tube)

Tip: teff and amaranth are available in both grain and flour form.

How to: drying your own beans is easy to do. Allow beans to dry on the vine. Pick when they are sufficiently dry (they will rattle) and crackly. To quickly shell the beans, place them in a burlap bag and whack the bag against the ground. Empty the contents of the bag and separate the beans from the chafe. Pasteurize/sterilize beans to kill any insects or eggs by placing in a single layer, on a cookie sheet, in a preheated 160° oven, for 30 minutes. Store in an airtight container in a cool, dry place.

Now Add Some Creativity!

Bean Soup VG GF   Serves 6 to 8

1 minced onion
1 minced red pepper
2 minced ribs celery
2 minced carrots
2 - 3 T. olive oil
1 - 2 cloves minced garlic
2 T. tomato paste
2 T. vermouth
2 tsp. smoked hot paprika, or to taste
2 bay leaves
2 - 3 sprigs of fresh thyme, whole
4 C. brined navy or white beans
4 C. vegetable stock (or chicken or ham for non-vegetarian version)
2 - 4 C. water
1 (14.5 oz.) can diced fire-roasted tomatoes
Apple cider vinegar to taste
1 large bunch of either curly or Lacinato kale, cleaned and ribs discarded, and cut into bite-size pieces
Kosher or coarse salt and freshly ground pepper to taste
Grated Romano cheese, if desired

Cover beans with cold water. Add 2 to 3 tablespoons kosher salt. Soak 2 to 3 hours. Drain and rinse well. Place in slow cooker, cover with boiling water and cook on high until barely tender, usually 2 to 3 hours. Drain. Sauté onion, celery, carrots and red pepper in olive oil for 4 to 5 minutes in large pot. Add garlic and cook for 30 seconds. Add tomato paste, cook for 1 to 2 minutes. Add paprika and cook for 30 seconds. De-glaze with vermouth. Add beans, tomatoes, broth, and 2 cups water. Bring to slow simmer on stove, adding more water as needed. When beans are tender (usually 15 to 20 minutes), add kale and cook for 5 minutes. Remove bay leaves and thyme sprigs and discard. Add vinegar, salt and pepper to taste. Serve with grated Romano cheese and crusty bread.

Dried Bean Soup GF DF   Serves 6 to 8

1 lb. dried beans, any variety
4 onion, chopped
2 cloves garlic, chopped
3 T. olive oil
3 T. bacon grease
2 branches fresh (or 1 T. dry) rosemary
2 bay leaves
8 C. chicken or vegetable stock (see Bulb, Roots & Tubers chapter for recipe)
Salt to taste
Pepper to taste

Soak beans overnight. In soup pot, heat olive oil and bacon grease. Sauté onions and garlic over medium heat until soft. Add remaining ingredients and simmer 45 to 60 minutes or until beans are soft. Using an immersion blender or hand mixer, briefly blend the soup in the pot, just until chunky, not puréed.

To serve, spoon into bowls and top with a drizzle of olive oil, parsley or dollop of sour cream.

(i) **Tip:** not keen on using bacon grease? Try substituting olive oil or, better yet, bacon-flavored olive oil, available on-line.

Polish Mushroom & Barley Christmas Soup GF   Serves 8

1 lb. cleaned and thickly sliced cremini mushrooms
1 oz. dried smoked Polish mushrooms, soaked in hot water for 20 minutes
Olive oil
1 large onion, chopped
2 stalks celery, chopped
2 cloves garlic, minced
2 - 3 sprigs fresh thyme
1 - 2 fresh bay leaves
1 C. barley
2 qt. chicken or beef broth
Smoked hot paprika, to taste
Salt and black pepper, to taste

> *This soup is often served in Polish homes on Christmas Eve.*
> *- Linda Bondurant*

Parsley for garnish
1 - 2 C. sour cream or yogurt, to taste

Sauté the cremini mushrooms in 2 to 3 tablespoons olive oil in a large heavy pot until caramelized, about 15 minutes. Remove from pot. Sauté onion and celery until limp. Add garlic and paprika and stir for 30 seconds. Strain Polish mushrooms in a sieve lined with paper towels. Save liquid. Chop mushrooms. Add barley, both kinds of mushrooms, bay leaves, and thyme to pot. Add broth and mushroom liquid until covered. If you need more liquid, add water. Bring to boil, and then reduce flame to simmer for 20 minutes. Check for doneness of barley and season with salt and black pepper if needed. When barley is done, check for seasonings again. Remove thyme sprigs and bay leaves. Add sour cream or yogurt to taste. Garnish with chopped parsley.

Tip: smoked paprika and Polish mushrooms are available at Buck's Fifth Avenue spice store in Olympia, Washington or online at culinaryexotica@gmail.com.

Tabbouleh VG DF   Serves 6

1 C. cracked (bulgur) wheat
1 cucumber, chopped
3 green onions
2 ripe tomatoes, seeded and chopped
2 T. chopped chives
1 C. chopped flat-leaf parsley
½ C. olive oil
Juice of 2 lemons (about ½ cup)
Salt and pepper to taste

Soak wheat in 1 quart water for 15 minutes or overnight. Drain and squeeze out excess moisture by tying in a clean kitchen towel. Combine with remaining ingredients. Set aside to marinate for 2 to 3 hours before serving.

Fact: bulgur is a Middle Eastern staple that sounds more exotic than it is. This cereal grain is what is left after wheat kernels have been steamed, dried, and crushed. It has been a food staple for years, because it offers an inexpensive source of protein.

Cedars-Inspired Lentil Soup VG GF DF   Serves 8 to 10

1 onion, chopped
5 (or more) cloves garlic, pressed or chopped
1 carrot, thinly sliced
2 stalks celery sliced less thinly than the carrot, but still pretty thin
2 yellow potatoes, cubed
1 C. red lentils
1 C. green lentils
Oil for the pan
1 tsp. cinnamon
1 tsp. cumin
1 tsp. garam masala spice blend
½ tsp. cardamom
8 C. water
4 bouillon cubes dissolved in some boiled water <u>or</u> 8 cups good stock
1 bunch chard, coarsely chopped
1 - 2 lemons or limes, juiced

Sauté the onion and garlic in some oil in your soup pot. Next add celery, then carrots and potatoes. Sauté briefly, then add your broth/stock. Add lentils and spices. Stir well. Bring to a boil, then turn down to simmer. Let soup cook until the lentils are soft. Add the chard and cook 5 more minutes. Add the lemon or lime juice. Stir. Taste it. Add more sour, if you need to. Accept praise from your dinner guests!

> *This lentil soup was inspired by the soup I had at a restaurant in the University District in Seattle called Cedars. I ate there frequently because it was so delicious and made me feel healthy and nourished. It took me a long time to figure out an approximation of the spices they used, but I think I got it pretty close. The last time I ate there, the lentil soup was totally different than it used to be, so now if I want a taste of the good old days, I have to make it myself.*
>
> *- Erin Majors*

ⓘ **Note:** using the 2 kinds of lentils is crucial for the texture. If you don't care so much about the texture, you can just use one or the other.

ⓘ **Tip:** don't have garam masala in your spice rack? A combination of ½ teaspoon each cumin and paprika, plus ¼ teaspoon each cinnamon, cayenne pepper, crumbled bay leaves, and ⅛ teaspoon ground cloves comes close.

Quinoa Salad   VG GF DF   Serves 6

2 C. cooked and cooled quinoa, any color
1 block extra firm tofu, cubed and baked (toss with oil and bake at 400° until toasted, about 15 minutes)
2 T. minced shallots, or to taste (rinse in cold water for a milder taste)
1 chopped red pepper
1 peeled and seeded chopped English cucumber
2 C. cooked black beans
1 large mango or 2 C. chopped fresh pineapple
½ C. olive or canola oil
3 T. rice or champagne vinegar or more, to taste
1 T. fresh grated ginger
1 T. fish or soy sauce
Sriracha or other hot sauce to taste
Salt and black pepper to taste
½ tsp. sugar
2 - 3 limes
1 bunch chopped cilantro

Combine quinoa, shallots, pepper, cucumber, beans, and fruit in large bowl. Whisk together (or shake in large jar) oil, vinegar, ginger, soy or fish sauce, Sriracha or hot sauce, salt, black pepper, sugar. Pour half over ingredients and keep adding dressing until moist. Squeeze limes over top, add cilantro and mix well. Cover and let sit for 1 hour at room temperature, or put in fridge. Serve at room temperature.

ⓘ **Fact:** the recently rediscovered ancient grain, quinoa was once called "*the gold of the Incas,*" valued by their warriors for increasing stamina. Not only is quinoa high in protein, but the protein it supplies is complete protein, meaning it includes all nine of the essential amino acids.

Ancient Grains Polenta with Puttanesca Sauce VG GF

1 C. millet
1 C. amaranth or teff (or use ½ cup of each)
4 C. vegetable stock (see Bulb, Roots & Tubers chapter for recipe)
½ tsp. salt
¾ C. grated Parmesan cheese

Combine millet, amaranth, teff, and water in a saucepan with a tight-fitting lid. Bring to a boil, then reduce the heat to a simmer and cook, covered, for 25 minutes. Lift the lid and stir it a few times during cooking. After 30 minutes, it should be a thick, porridge-like consistency. (If molding into polenta cakes, keep stirring and cooking another five minutes until it forms a more solid mass). Stir in Parmesan, salt & pepper.

> *For a vegan version of this recipe, replace the parmesan cheese with 2 tablespoons miso and 4 tablespoons brewer's or nutritional yeast.*
>
> *__Ingrid Lundin*

Serve as a porridge <u>or</u> make into polenta cakes. For cakes, scrape the polenta into a lightly oiled 9x13 baking pan and smooth the top. Chill in the refrigerator for 3 hours, then unmold onto a cutting board. Slice into triangles or bars. Heat oven to 450° and while the oven is heating, put a heavy baking pan in the oven. Take the pan out and drizzle 1 tablespoon of olive oil into the pan. Place the polenta slices in the oil, then drizzle another tablespoon of oil over the top of the polenta. Bake for 5 minutes, then turn slices over with spatula and bake another 5 minutes until edges are crispy. Serve topped with Puttanesca Sauce (recipe follows).

ⓘ **Tip:** millet, amaranth and teff can be found at organic/health food stores and food co-ops in bulk or packaged. They can sometimes be found in the bulk foods aisle of larger grocery stores. The Bob's Red Mill brand of these grains can often be found in grocery stores, usually on the baking aisle where all-purpose wheat and other flours are located.

ⓘ **Fact:** "grains" such as quinoa, amaranth, and spelt are called "ancient" because they've been around, unchanged, for millennia. By contrast, corn, rice and modern varieties of wheat have been bred selectively over thousands of years to look and taste much different from their distant ancestors.

Puttanesca Sauce for Ancient Grains Polenta QE VG GF DF

½ C. low-sodium vegetable broth
1 C. diced white onion
4 cloves garlic, minced
½ tsp. crushed red pepper
1 T. no-salt-added tomato paste
2 (28-ounce) cans whole tomatoes, drained and chopped or 6 cups diced plum tomatoes
¼ C. pitted Kalamata olives, chopped
2 T. capers, rinsed and drained
3 T. chopped fresh basil
3 T. chopped fresh parsley
2 T. fresh minced oregano
1 - 2 cans white beans, if desired, for protein

Heat broth to a simmer in a large skillet over medium-high heat. Add onion, garlic and red pepper and cook 4 minutes or until onions are translucent and beginning to brown. Stir in tomato paste and cook 1 minute, stirring. Add tomatoes, olives and capers, and beans and bring to a simmer. Reduce heat to medium and cook 20 minutes, stirring occasionally. Remove from heat and stir in basil, parsley, and oregano. Serve over polenta (or pasta).

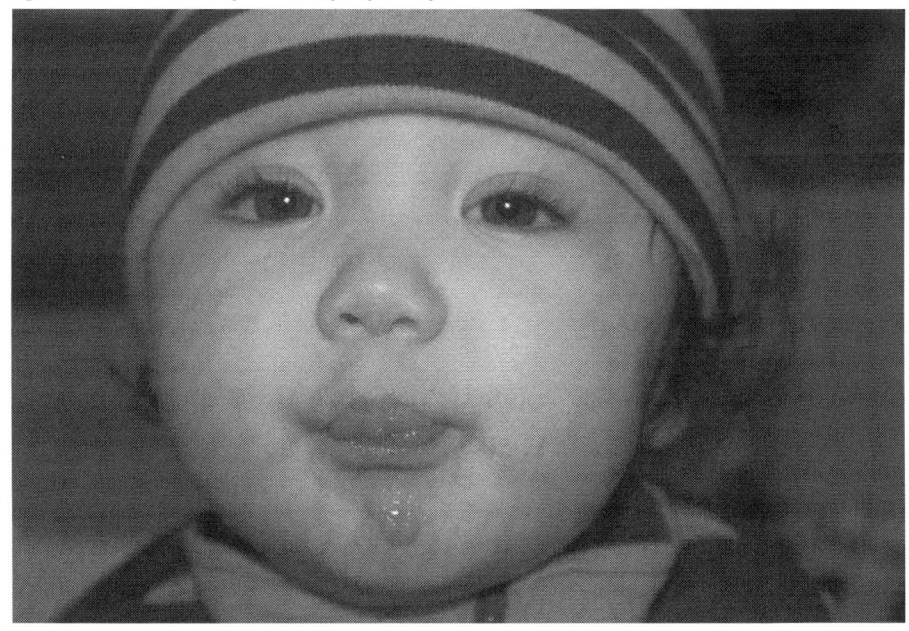

Polenta with Butter and Cheese QE VG GF   Serves 4

4 C. water or stock, boiling
1 tsp. salt
1 C. coarse cornmeal (polenta)
½ C. grated Parmesan cheese
1 T. butter

Add salt to boiling water. Whisking constantly with a strong wire whisk, gradually pour the cornmeal into the water in a steady stream. Whisk out any lumps. Continue whisking constantly until mixture thickens. Lower heat to a very low simmer and continue to stir occasionally using a wooden spoon until full thickening is achieved, about 25 minutes. Stir in cheese and butter; remove from heat. Serve immediately, or allow to cool for grilling or frying.

ⓘ **Tip:** vary the taste of this polenta by adding fresh herbs from the garden. Basil and thyme work nicely.

Lentil & Quinoa Breakfast Patties VG GF DF

2½ C. lentils, soaked and cooked (start with 1 cup dry)
1 C. quinoa, soaked and cooked (start with ½ cup dry)
½ red onion, chopped
1/3 C. carrot, chopped
2 T. ground golden flax
1½ tsp. fine ground sea salt
1 tsp. paprika
3 cloves garlic, minced
1 tsp. fennel seed, roughly chopped
1½ tsp. sucanat
1 T. fresh sage, chopped fine
1 T. fresh marjoram, chopped fine
¼ tsp. red pepper flakes (or more if you like more heat)
1 tsp. fresh ground black pepper
3 tsp. coconut oil (virgin, cold-pressed)

Cook lentils and quinoa and set aside. Both can be prepared a day or two ahead and kept in the refrigerator in an airtight glass container until ready to use.

Place 2 teaspoons coconut oil in pan and heat to medium-high. Add chopped onion and carrots and brown for about 10 to 15 minutes. While the vegetables are cooking, chop the fresh herbs, fennel seeds, and garlic; set aside.

Mix the salt, paprika, garlic, fennel, sucanat, sage, marjoram, red pepper and black pepper in a small bowl. Once the vegetables are browned place them, along with the flax and herbs in a food processor. Add the cooked quinoa and lentils. Pulse the food processor just enough to break up the lentils, quinoa and vegetables so they start to stick together, about 20 pulses. Don't over process.

Form into patties and brown on each side in a skillet. You can also just brown the mixture as crumbles and use to replace sausage in many recipes. Store in an airtight glass container in the refrigerator or freezer. Reheat in an oven or skillet.

Tip: substitute brown sugar or turbinado/raw sugar for sucanat (a minimally refined form of cane sugar), if you cannot find it at grocery or organic foods stores.

Oatcakes QE VG DF

Makes 1 oatcake

1 egg
½ C. oatmeal
½ C. hot water

Soak oatmeal in the hot water for 5 minutes. Mix the egg and oatmeal. Lightly grease a skillet with vegetable oil. Form the oatmeal mixture into a pancake and fry on one side until browned. Turn and brown the other side. Can be served with applesauce, other fruit sauce, or butter and syrup.

Information: Scottish soldiers in the 14th century carried a metal plate and a sack of oatmeal. They would heat the plate over the fire, moisten a bit of oatmeal, and make a cake to "comfort the stomach" (http://outremer.co.uk/feasting.html).

Information: oats contain a wide array of vitamins, minerals, and antioxidants and are a good source of protein, complex carbohydrates, and iron.

Chocolate Peanut Butter Pie with Teff Crust VG GF DF

Crust:
2 C. teff flour
½ C. maple syrup
2 T. peanut butter (or almond butter)
5 tsp. melted coconut oil
¼ tsp. sea salt
Almond milk, if needed for moisture

Filling:
1½ C. dark chocolate (chips or bar)
16 oz. non-dairy yogurt or silken tofu (or try plain coconut yogurt to make soy- free)
3 T. peanut butter (or more!)
2 tsp. vanilla
Optional stir-ins: roughly chopped chocolate, shredded unsweetened coconut (small flakes)

Pre-heat oven to 375°. Lightly oil a 9-inch pie pan.

To make crust, put all crust ingredients in a medium-sized bowl and stir until well combined. If a little more moisture is needed, use almond milk to moisten the dough. Transfer dough to the prepared pie pan, and use a spoon or your fingers to press it out into an even layer over the bottom and sides of the pan. Poke a few holes in the dough with a fork, and then bake for about 10 minutes, until it loses its shine. Let the crust cool while making the filling. Note: leave the oven on if you want to bake the pie as described at the end of the recipe.

To make the filling, melt the chocolate in a double-boiler or saucepan on the stovetop over medium-low heat, stirring occasionally. A metal bowl fitted snugly on top of a saucepan works well as a double boiler. Melting can also be done in a microwave. While the chocolate is melting, stir the yogurt, peanut butter, and vanilla together in a bowl. Pour in the melted chocolate and stir to mix. Transfer the melted chocolate and peanut butter mixture to a bowl, add the vanilla and yogurt, and stir to mix. If you are using optional stir-ins, mix in now.

> *So decadent...and yet gluten-free, soy-free, vegan. This teff crust is delicious, and could work as a base in savory dishes as well (quiche!) by reducing the amount of maple syrup.*
> *- Ingrid Lundin*

Note: if using silken tofu, add the tofu, peanut butter, vanilla, and chocolate to a food processor and blend until smooth.

Pour filling into crust and smooth the top. Place in the refrigerator to set. If you like, the pie can be baked for about 5 minutes, until the edges of the filling darken slightly, before refrigerating. Whether baked or not, refrigerating the pie is needed to help the pie set up before serving, otherwise the filling will be like pudding. Serve with Coconut Whipped Cream (recipe follows).

Tip: teff flour can be found at organic/health food stores in bulk or packaged. Bob's Red Mill brand can often be found in larger grocery stores.

Tip: to make this recipe peanut-free, try other kinds of nut butters such as hazelnut butter

Tip: replacing part of the teff flour with almond meal produces good results.

Coconut Whipped Cream   QE VG GF DF

1 can coconut milk (full fat, not light!)
¼ tsp. vanilla extract
2 - 3 tsp. sugar

Chill a mixing bowl in the refrigerator or freezer. Remove only the cream portion of the coconut milk from the can into the mixing bowl, being careful not to get any of the liquid from the can. Add the vanilla and sugar to the bowl, then beat on high with an electric beater until peaks are fluffy and firm. Chill in refrigerator for 10 minutes before serving.

Information: coconut milk is a nutrient-dense food containing calcium, omega-3 fats, fiber, and protein. There is no change in the chemical composition of the oils in coconut milk during cooking which means it doesn't lose its nutritional benefits.

Flourless Pancakes   VG GF DF

2/3 C. steel cut oats
1/3 C. buckwheat groats (or other grain such as millet)
1¼ C. non-dairy milk
1 egg
¼ tsp. sea salt
2 T. unrefined cane sugar (or honey, maple syrup, etc.)
1 tsp. baking powder
½ tsp. grated nutmeg

Combine oats, buckwheat, milk, and water in a blender jar. Cover and soak overnight or 6 to 8 hours in the refrigerator. Put blender jar on the base, add remaining ingredients and blend until smooth. Add a little water or more non-dairy milk, if needed. Preheat oiled griddle. Pour about 1/4 cup batter onto the griddle and cook for about 2 minutes on each side or until golden. Repeat until all batter is used. Keep finished pancakes warm in the oven until ready to serve.

Note: try using a combination of 1/2 cup yogurt plus 3/4 cup water in place of the non-dairy milk to soak the grains.

Gluten Free Whole Grain Muffins   VG GF   Makes about 15 muffins

350 grams whole-grain flour mix (see note next page)
½ tsp. baking soda
¼ tsp. baking powder
180 grams dark brown sugar (or substitute sucanat or coconut sugar)
1 tsp. kosher salt
2 eggs
300 grams buttermilk (or substitute soy or rice milk)
100 grams grapeseed oil (or substitute olive oil, coconut oil or melted butter)
Handful of dried fruit (figs, apricots, raisins, or apples)
Handful of nuts (walnuts, pecans, pine nuts, or pistachios)

Preheat the oven to 350°. Thoroughly grease a large muffin tin. Combine the flour, baking soda, baking powder, sugar, and salt in a large bowl. Whisk together to combine and aerate.

In another bowl, whisk together the eggs, buttermilk, and grapeseed oil until well combined. Add to the dry ingredients, blending with a rubber spatula until almost fully combined. Throw in the figs and walnuts; continue stirring until all trace of flour is gone. Fill muffin tins 3/4 full and place in oven to bake for 25 to 35 minutes. Muffins should be nicely browned with a bit of a crunch; the top should spring back to the touch and a knife inserted should come out cleanly.

ⓘ**Note:** to make your own whole-grain flour mix, choose 700 grams of any combination of the following flours - almond, amaranth, brown rice, buckwheat, corn, millet, oat, quinoa, sorghum, sweet brown rice, and teff. Find your own favorite combination, then throw in 300 grams of any combination of the following starches - arrowroot, cornstarch, potato starch, tapioca flour, and white rice flour. After combining the 700 grams of whole-grain flours with the 300 grams of starches (i.e., 70% whole grains and 30% starches), store in a large container. Shake to keep blended.

ⓘ**Tip:** if a food scale is not available to measure by weight, us a metric conversion chart to determine the amount to measure by capacity, i.e., by cups, tablespoons, etc.

ⓘ**Tip:** try substituting a chia seed slurry for the eggs (1 teaspoon ground chia seeds plus 3 tablespoons hot water, per egg) to make an egg-free version of these muffins.

Shoots & Stems

Basic Ways of Cooking & Serving

Vegetable	Preparation	Cooking Time	Ways to Serve
Asparagus	Snap off tough end of spears; boil or steam until crispy tender. For roasting, toss with olive oil, salt, and pepper.	Drop spears into boiling water; reduce to simmer and cook 5-8 minutes. To conserve nutrients, cook in a steamer basket. Arrange spears on baking sheet or in roasting pan; roast in 400° over 20-25 minutes, shaking pan a few times during roasting period.	Buttered with salt and pepper. Vary with dash of lemon juice, garlic powder, minced onion, or chives. For roasted, serve as is.
Fennel	Remove stalks from bulb by cutting across bulb where color changes from green to white. Cut off root end. Slice or chop, then sauté or roast.	Mix with other vegetables (potato, carrots, turnips, etc.); coat with oil and favorite herbs, then roast for 45 minutes in 375° oven. Sauté in small amount of cooking oil until golden brown and soft.	Add salt and pepper or season with fresh herbs to taste.
Rhubarb	For most recipes, remove leaves and coarse ends, then slice the stalks into the size of pieces recipe requires.	Follow desired recipe.	Rhubarb cooks down into wonderful sauces, desserts, and condiments.

ⓘ **Information:** discard rhubarb leaves, as they are poisonous; because of rhubarb's high acid content, use nonreactive cookware (enamel, glass, or stainless steel).

ⓘ **Tip:** rhubarb stores quite well in the freezer; just wash and cut into manageable pieces, then store in freezer bags to use until you have fresh rhubarb again.

ⓘ **Tip:** whatever size asparagus stalks you choose, for optimal freshness the tips should be closed.

ⓘ **Tip:** save fennel stalks and boil them with other vegetables to make vegetable broth.

ⓘ **Tip:** to store fennel, wrap in plastic and refrigerate. It keeps for just a few days; the flavor fades as it dries out.

Now Add Some Creativity!

Asparagus, Spinach, & Strawberry Salad VG GF DF   Serves 6 to 8

1 lb. asparagus, trimmed and cut into 1-inch pieces
½ lb. spinach leaves
½ lb. strawberries, hulled and sliced
½ C. toasted walnuts (to toast, bake in 350° oven until golden, about 10 min.)
3 T. olive oil, divided into 1T. and 2 T.
2 T. raspberry or balsamic vinegar
¼ tsp. salt
Pepper

Preheat oven to 400°. Pour the 1 tablespoon of oil onto a baking sheet; add asparagus, sprinkle with the salt. Mix to coat, then spread in a single layer to bake. Stir often until asparagus stems are tender when pierced, about 15-20 minutes. Let cool about 15 minutes. In the meantime, put the vinegar and remaining oil in a screw-top jar and shake vigorously to blend. Place spinach, strawberries, toasted walnuts and the cooled asparagus into serving bowl. Pour dressing over and toss to coat. Add more salt, if desired, and pepper to taste.

Asparagus with Balsamic Tomatoes QE VG GF   Serves 4

1 lb. asparagus, trimmed
2 tsp. olive oil
1½ C. grape tomatoes, halved
½ tsp. minced garlic
2 T. balsamic vinegar
¼ tsp. salt
3 T. goat cheese (or soft cheese of your choice)
½ tsp. black pepper

Cook asparagus in boiling water until crisp-tender, about 2 minutes. Drain. Heat oil in a skillet over medium-high heat. Add tomatoes and garlic; cook 5 minutes. Stir in vinegar and cook 3 more minutes. Stir in salt. Arrange asparagus on serving platter. Top with tomato mixture and sprinkle with cheese and pepper.

Sesame-Ginger Glazed Asparagus   QE VG GF DF   Serves 4

1 lb. asparagus, trimmed
1 T. soy sauce
1 tsp. honey
1 tsp. lime juice
1 tsp. minced fresh ginger
½ tsp. minced garlic
Sesame seeds

Cook asparagus in boiling water until crisp-tender, about 2 minutes. Drain. Combine remaining ingredients, except sesame seeds, and microwave on High for 2 minutes. Place asparagus on a serving platter, drizzle with glaze & sprinkle with sesame seeds.

Roasted Asparagus with Orange Sauce   QE VG GF DF   Serves 4

1 lb. asparagus, trimmed
2 tsp. olive oil
1 tsp. grated orange rind
¼ C. fresh orange juice
2 T. lemon juice
¼ C. cold water
2 tsp. cornstarch

Preheat oven to 475°. Arrange asparagus spears in a single layer on a baking sheet. Brush with the olive oil. Bake for 7 to 9 minutes or until tender, turning every few minutes. Transfer to a serving platter and keep warm. Combine orange rind, orange juice, and lemon juice in a small saucepan. Bring to a boil over medium heat. Combine the water and cornstarch, stirring until smooth, then slowly add it to the orange juice mixture. Cook, stirring constantly, until the mixture is thickened. Cook 1 minute more, then remove from the heat and spoon evenly over the asparagus. Serve immediately.

ⓘ**Information:** asparagus are low in calories and loaded with vitamins and minerals. They are a good source of folic acid and vitamins A, B, and C; also a fair source of calcium and fiber.

ⓘ**Fact:** asparagus begins to lose its sweetness as soon as it's picked, so use right away.

Fennel Mediterranean Salad   VG GF   Serves 10 (1 cup servings)

3 T. red wine vinegar
2 T. water
3 T. olive oil
2 tsp. finely chopped fresh oregano or marjoram
1 tsp. Dijon mustard
½ tsp. salt
1 tsp. pepper
2 cloves garlic, minced
2 C. sliced fennel bulb (about 1 medium)
1½ C. thinly sliced red onion
1 C. pitted Italian style ripe olives, halved
¾ C. chopped flat-leaf parsley
½ C. crumbled feta cheese
1 (15-oz.) can cannellini beans, drained and rinsed
6 Roma style tomatoes, quartered
Sunflower seeds for garnish

Place first 8 ingredients in a screw-top jar and shake to blend. Combine remaining ingredients, except sunflower seeds, in a large bowl. Drizzle dressing over and toss until well combined. Sprinkle sunflower seeds over top, cover, and chill at least 1 hour.

Roasted Fennel and Carrots   VG GF   Serves 8

4 fennel bulbs, cut vertically into ½ inch wide strips
2 tsp. chopped fennel fronds
2 large carrots, peeled and cut diagonally into 1/3 inch slices
2 tsp. chopped fresh thyme
½ C. hard Italian cheese (Parmesan, Romano, Asiago, or Pecorino)
1/3 C. olive oil

Preheat oven to 375°. Lightly oil a 13 x 9 inch baking dish. Layer the sliced fennel and carrots in the pan, sprinkling the layers with salt and pepper. Sprinkle top with thyme and cheese, then drizzle with olive oil. Bake until vegetables are tender and top is golden brown, about 75 minutes. To serve, sprinkle with fronds.

Fennel Slaw with Orange Vinaigrette   QE VG GF DF   Serves 8

2 T. olive oil
½ T. wine vinegar
1 tsp. grated orange peel
2½ to 3 tsp. fresh orange juice
½ tsp. sea salt
⅛ tsp. freshly ground pepper
⅛ tsp. crushed red pepper
2 small to medium fennel bulbs with stalks (about 2 lbs.)
1 C. orange sections (about 1 large orange)
¼ C. coarsely chopped pitted green olives

Combine the first 7 ingredients in a bowl. Trim tough outer leaves from fennel; remove and discard stalks, saving the feathery fronds. Mince the feathery fronds to measure 1 cup. Cut fennel bulb in half lengthwise, discarding the core. Thinly slice the bulb, lengthwise. Add fronds, fennel slices, and orange sections to the bowl and toss gently to combine and coat all ingredients with the dressing. Sprinkle with olives.

Fennel, Cabbage, and Carrot Slaw   QE VG GF   Serves 5 or 6

1½ C. very thinly sliced fennel (1 fennel bulb)
9 C. thinly sliced cabbage (about 1 lb. of cabbage)
1 small, thinly sliced onion
1 medium, coarsely shredded carrot
6 T. mayonnaise
¼ C. sour cream
1 T. fresh lemon juice
¼ tsp. sugar
¼ tsp. hot pepper sauce (like Tabasco)

Combine fennel, cabbage, carrot, and onion in a bowl. Whisk together the mayonnaise, sour cream, lemon juice, sugar and hot sauce. Add dressing to the fennel-cabbage mixture and toss to coat. Season to taste with salt and pepper. Refrigerate at least one hour and up to two hours, tossing occasionally. Transfer to a serving bowl and enjoy!

Fennel & Cauliflower Gratin QE VG   Serves 8

1 large fennel bulb, trimmed, cut into ¼-inch slices
½ C. fennel fronds, chopped
1 head cauliflower, broken into florets
4 T. butter
2 T. flour
½ tsp. salt
⅛ tsp. ground nutmeg
½ C. cream
4 oz. shredded Swiss or Gruyere cheese
¾ C. soft bread crumbs
¼ C. grated Parmesan cheese

Melt butter in a large skillet over medium-high heat. Add cauliflower and sauté 4 minutes. Add sliced fennel and sauté another 4 minutes. Remove from heat. Sprinkle with flour, salt, and nutmeg; add fennel fronds and toss gently together. Spoon cauliflower-fennel mixture into a 2-qt. gratin or baking dish. Pour cream over the mixture, the sprinkle with remaining ingredients - Swiss cheese, bread crumbs and Parmesan cheese. Bake in a preheated 450°oven until top is browned and crisp, about 20 minutes.

ⓘ**Tip:** try baking this dish in individual ramekins.

ⓘ**Information:** the bulb, stalks, leaves and seeds of fennel are all edible.

ⓘ**Information:** fennel is an excellent source of potassium, vitamin C, and fiber and a good source of folic acid, phosphorous, iron, calcium, magnesium, and manganese.

Rhubarb Crumble QE VG

Serves 6 to 8

Fruit Base:
4 C. rhubarb, cut into 1-inch pieces
1 C. water
1 C. sugar
1 tsp. vanilla
2 T. cornstarch

Topping:
1 C. flour
¾ C. rolled oats
1 C. brown sugar
½ C. butter, room temperature (i.e., soft)
1 tsp. cinnamon

Mix together topping ingredients. Press half of this mixture into an 8-inch pan. Cover with rhubarb. In a saucepan, mix together the cornstarch, sugar, water and vanilla. Cook over medium heat, stirring until thick and clear. Pour over the rhubarb. Cover rhubarb with the remaining topping. Bake 1 hour at 350°. To serve (warm or cooled), spoon into small dishes and top with a dollop of whipped cream, if desired.

ⓘ**Information:** rhubarb provides a good source of vitamin C, fiber, and calcium. It is also a fair source of potassium.

Rhubarb Walnut Bread QE VG

Makes 2 loaves

1 C. brown sugar
½ C. granulated sugar
2/3 C. vegetable oil
2 eggs
1 C. milk
1½ C. diced rhubarb
1 tsp. vanilla
1 tsp. salt
2½ C. flour
1½ tsp. baking powder

½ tsp. baking soda
½ C. chopped walnuts

Mix together both sugars with the oil; add eggs and mix well. Blend in the milk, then add the remaining ingredients, mixing well. Pour into two 9 x 5 loaf pans. Top each with a teaspoon of melted butter and a tablespoon of sugar. Bake at 350° for one hour or until done.

Rhubarb Muffins QE VG

Makes about 18 muffins

Muffin batter:
½ C. butter, softened
1 C. packed brown sugar
½ C. granulated sugar
1 egg
2 C. flour
1 tsp. baking powder
½ tsp. baking soda
⅛ tsp. salt
1 C. sour cream
3 C. chopped fresh rhubarb

Topping:
½ C. chopped nuts (walnuts, pecans, etc.)
¼ C. packed brown sugar
1 tsp. cinnamon
1 T. cold butter, cut into very small pieces

For the muffin batter, cream sugars and butter together. Add egg and beat well. Combine flour, baking powder, baking soda, and salt. Add to creamed mixture alternating with sour cream until all dry ingredients and sour cream are blended in. Fold in the rhubarb. Fill paper-lined or greased muffin cups ¾ full. For the topping, combine the nuts, brown sugar, and cinnamon in a small bowl. Add butter pieces to the bowl. Work butter into the other ingredients until crumbly, using a fork or your fingers. Distribute this mixture over the tops of the muffins and bake at 350° for 20 to 25 minutes or until a toothpick inserted in muffin comes out clean. Cool 5 minutes before removing from pans.

Rhubarb Cookies QE VG

Makes about 4½ dozen

Cookie dough:
1 C. butter, softened
1 C. granulated sugar
1 C. packed brown sugar
4 eggs
4½ C. flour
1 tsp. baking soda
1 tsp. salt

Filling:
3½ C. chopped fresh rhubarb
1½ C. granulated sugar
6 T. cold water, divided (2 T. and 4 T.)
¼ C. cornstarch
1 tsp. vanilla

Cream together the butter and sugars. Add the eggs, one at a time, beating after each addition. Combine flour, baking soda, and salt, then gradually add to the creamed mixture. Mix well.

For filling, combine the rhubarb, sugar, and 2 tablespoons water in a large saucepan. Bring to a boil, then reduce heat and simmer uncovered for 10 minutes, stirring frequently. Combine cornstarch and remaining cold water in a small bowl, stirring until smooth. Stir into the rhubarb mixture. Bring to a boil and cook and stir for two minutes or until thickened. Remove from the heat and stir in the vanilla.

To make the cookies, drop the cookie dough by tablespoonfuls about 2 inches apart onto an ungreased baking sheet. Using the end of a wooden spoon handle, make an indentation in the center of each cookie and fill with a rounded teaspoonful of filling. Top with 1/2 teaspoon of dough, allowing some of the filling to show. Bake at 375° for 8 to 10 minutes or until lightly browned.

Tip: try substituting fig or other preserves for the rhubarb filling when rhubarb is not in season.

Rhubarb Sauce   QE VG GF DF

1 lb. rhubarb (about 3 ½ cups chopped in ½-inch pieces)
¼ - ½ C. sugar, depending on desired sweetness
¼ - ½ C. water
1 T. vegetable oil or butter

Put all ingredients in a small sized saucepan. Stir. Bring to a boil over medium heat, stirring occasionally. Turn down heat and simmer for about 10 minutes or until soft. Serve warm or chilled. Great over vanilla ice cream.

Tip: substitute fresh squeezed orange juice for part of the water; add some orange zest.

Tip: for a very smooth sauce, transfer from saucepan to a food processor or blender after cooking and process until smooth.

Rhubarb Marmalade   VG GF DF   Makes about 8 half-pints

6 C. chopped fresh rhubarb
6 C. sugar
2 medium oranges

Combine rhubarb and sugar in a large heavy saucepan. Grind the oranges, including the peels, in a food processor; add to the rhubarb mixture. Bring to a boil, then reduce the heat and simmer, uncovered, stirring often until the marmalade sheets from a spoon (turn spoon sideways). This will take about one hour.

Pour marmalade into hot sterilized jars, leaving ¼-inch headspace. Adjust caps. Process in a boiling-water bath for 10 minutes.

Fact: though actually a vegetable, rhubarb is treated more like fruit. It is typically made into such things as pies, tarts, preserves, and wine. It is very tart, and at its best when combined with berries.

Fact: rhubarb is native to western China where the earliest records of its use date back to 2700 B.C. The Chinese cultivated it for medicinal purposes.

Squash

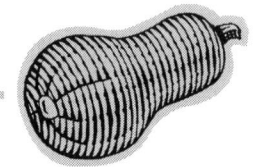

Basic Ways of Cooking & Serving

Vegetable	Preparation	Cooking Time	Ways to Serve
Pumpkin	Cut in half. Remove seeds and stringy interior. Cut in large pieces if baking, small pieces if boiling; pare.	Boil 25-30 minutes or bake at 400° for 1 hour (varies with size).	Mashed and seasoned with butter, salt, and pepper. Unseasoned for pie filling. Use in same way as sweet potatoes or squash.
Summer Squash Patty Pan, Crookneck, Zucchini	Remove stem and blossom ends. Remove large seeds (except in zucchini) and coarse fiber, if any. Leave whole, slice, or dice. Paring not necessary.	Boil whole 30-60 minutes; cut for 10-15. Bake whole at 350°, for 30-60 minutes, depending on squash type and size. Sauté until desired tenderness is reached.	Buttered with salt and pepper. Vary with marjoram, tarragon, or Parmesan cheese. Baked, mashed, sautéed.
Winter Squash Hubbard, Butternut, Acorn	Acorn - do not pare; cut in half; remove seeds and stringy interior. Brush with butter and seasonings before, during, or after baking. Other squash - pare, if desired; remove seeds and stringy interior; cut into serving size pieces.	Bake at 375° 40-60 minutes. Bake halves of acorn squash cut-side-down, turn after half of baking time. Bake covered for moist top, uncovered for crusty top. If cooking to use as an ingredient, may be boiled 25-30 minutes.	Baked, buttered, glazed, mashed. Spoon brown sugar into hollows last 15-30 minutes of baking. Scoop out and mash with cream, nutmeg, candied ginger, grated orange rind or orange juice.

Now Add Some Creativity!

Apple-Stuffed Acorn Squash　VG　GF

Serves 4

2 acorn squash
2 T. butter
2 medium apples, peeled and chopped
½ C. pecans or walnuts
½ C. apple juice
2 T. brown sugar
1 tsp. salt
½ tsp. nutmeg

Cut each squash in half lengthwise; remove and discard seeds and membranes. Place cut side down in a 13 x 9 baking pan. Add water to a depth of 1 inch. Cover and bake at 350° for 45 minutes.

Drain and return squash to the pan, cut side up. Set aside. Melt butter in a large skillet over medium heat. Add apples, nuts, apple juice, brown sugar, salt, and nutmeg. Cook, stirring occasionally, for 5 minutes. Spoon mixture into the squash halves. Bake an additional 15 minutes or until apples are tender.

Tip: substitute leftover Thanksgiving stuffing for the apple stuffing. Or simply place a tablespoon of butter and some brown sugar or maple syrup in each squash half; bake another 15 minutes, occasionally spooning the melted butter and sugar/syrup over the cut edges of the squash creating a nice caramelized glaze.

Creamy Butternut Squash, Carrot, & Apple Soup VG GF Serves 4 to 6

1 large butternut squash, pared, seeded and cubed
1 T. olive oil
1 small to medium onion, diced
1 large apple, pared and cubed
2 - 3 carrots, sliced
4 C. vegetable broth
2 tsp. cinnamon
½ tsp. nutmeg
½ tsp. curry powder
1 bay leaf
½ C. cream

Using a large soup pot, sauté the diced onion in olive oil. Once onions are soft and starting to brown, add the squash, apple, and carrots to the pot, along with the vegetable stock. Add the spices, stir, and bring to a boil. Once the soup begins to boil, cover and reduce heat to a simmer. Cook about 15 minutes, until the vegetables are very soft. Purée the soup to a creamy, thick consistency, using an immersion blender, food processor, or regular blender. You will need to purée in several batches if using a regular blender or food processor. Complete the soup by stirring in the half cup of cream. Bring back to a slight simmer, heat through, then serve.

Tip: for a lower calorie soup, try substituting almond milk for the cream in this recipe.

Butternut Squash "Lasagna"   VG GF DF

2 large butternut squash
1 1/3 C. raw walnuts, soaked 6 - 8 hours
1 2/3 C. raw cashews, soaked 2 hours
1½ tsp. fine ground sea salt
1 1/3 T. fresh lemon juice
2 cloves garlic
2 C. water
Lentil & Quinoa Breakfast Patties, crumbled (recipe follows)
Easy Tomato Sauce (recipe follows)
Fresh ground black pepper for seasoning
Fine ground sea salt for seasoning
Fresh chopped sage (optional)

Prepare the *Lentil & Quinoa Breakfast Patties* and *Easy Tomato Sauce* (recipes follow) and set aside. Preheat oven to 350°. Cut the squash in half, remove the seeds, then slice lengthwise into ⅛-inch thick pieces, using a very sharp knife or mandoline. Slice off the skin from the slices (or peel before slicing). Set aside.

Make walnut-cashew "cheese" by placing walnuts, cashews, sea salt, lemon juice, garlic, and water in a blender and mixing until thoroughly creamy. Pour into a bowl and set aside. Spoon some of the tomato sauce into the bottom of a casserole dish. Layer in the squash slices, doing your best to not overlap but create a tight layer. Season with pepper and salt. Spoon on a layer of "cheese" and spread it over the squash. Sprinkle on a layer of lentil-quinoa crumbles. Make another layer of squash, add the seasonings, spread on more tomato sauce followed by more "cheese" and crumbles. Repeat layering until the top of the casserole dish is reached, ending with "cheese" and crumbles. Place in the oven and bake uncovered for 40 minutes. Remove from oven and check for doneness - a knife inserted into the lasagna should easily go through; squash should be firm but not uncooked. When done, remove from the oven and allow to cool significantly before serving. Store in an airtight glass container in the refrigerator for up to 7 days. Reheat in the oven or eat cold.

ⓘ**Information:** nuts, seeds and legumes are packed with healthy fats, protein and minerals that are more easily assimilated into the body if soaked before using.

To complete the Butternut Squash Lasagna use Lentil & Quinoa Breakfast Patties and Easy Tomato Sauce recipes that follow:

Lentil & Quinoa Breakfast Patties   VG GF DF

2½ C. lentils, soaked and cooked (start with 1 cup dry)
1 C. quinoa, soaked and cooked (start with ½ cup dry)
½ red onion, chopped
1/3 C. carrot, chopped
2 T. ground golden flax
1½ tsp. fine ground sea salt
1 tsp. paprika
3 cloves garlic, minced
1 tsp. fennel seed, roughly chopped
1½ tsp. sucanat (brown sugar or turbinado/raw sugar can be substituted)
1 T. fresh sage, chopped fine
1 T. fresh marjoram, chopped fine
¼ tsp. red pepper flakes (or more if you like more heat)
1 tsp. fresh ground black pepper
3 tsp. coconut oil (virgin, cold-pressed)

Cook lentils and quinoa and set aside. Both can be prepared a day or two ahead and kept in the refrigerator in an airtight glass container until ready to use. Place 2 teaspoons coconut oil in pan and heat to medium-high. Add chopped onion and carrots and brown for about 10 to 15 minutes. While the vegetables are cooking, chop the fresh herbs, fennel seeds, and garlic; set aside. Mix the salt, paprika, garlic, fennel, sucanat, sage, marjoram, red pepper and black pepper in a small bowl. Once the vegetables are browned place them, along with the flax and herbs in a food processor. Add the cooked quinoa and lentils. Pulse the food processor just enough to break up the lentils, quinoa and vegetables so they start to stick together, about 20 pulses. Don't over process. Form into patties and brown on each side in a skillet. You can also just brown the mixture as crumbles and use to replace sausage in many recipes. Store in an airtight glass container in the refrigerator or freezer. Reheat in an oven or skillet.

Easy Tomato Sauce QE VG GF DF

1 T. cold-pressed, virgin coconut oil
½ red onion, chopped
3 stalks celery, chopped
2 carrots, peeled
5 large tomatoes, blanched
2 - 4 cloves garlic, minced
2 C. water
Fine ground sea salt, to taste
Fresh ground black pepper, to taste
Optional herbs - fresh basil, parsley, and/or oregano

Chop all the vegetables and put them in a large stock pot that has been coated with coconut oil. Cook over medium heat, stirring often. After 15 minutes, add the garlic and cook another 5 minutes until browned. In the meantime, blanch the tomatoes in a large saucepan of boiling water. Remove tomatoes from the water, peel, and add to the vegetables, along with 2 cups water. If using herbs, add to the sauce at this time and simmer together for about 10 minutes. Transfer cooked sauce to a blender and mix until thoroughly puréed, then transfer back to the stock pot. Season with salt and pepper to taste. Keep warm if you are going to use right away or store in an airtight glass container in the refrigerator or freezer.

Squash with Kale and Beans VG GF DF   Serves 4 to 6

2 Delicata squash, halved and seeded (acorn, small pumpkin or butternut also work)
2 - 4 T. olive oil
2 T. honey or maple syrup
2 T. sherry vinegar
1 medium bunch curly kale, stemmed and cut in bite size pieces
Red pepper flakes to taste
2 T. shallot, minced
2 C. cooked beans (cannellini, pinto or cranberry)
Salt and black pepper

Cut squash into ½-inch moons and toss with olive oil on a large rimmed baking sheet. Roast at 400 ° for 15 minutes or until tender. Mix sweetener and vinegar.

Toss half the vinegar mix with the squash. Bake 5 minutes. Sauté shallots and pepper flakes in olive oil in large skillet. Turn off skillet. Add rest of vinegar mix to pan. Add kale and toss with salt and black pepper. Add beans and squash. You may want to add more vinegar or olive oil. Cover pan for 3 minutes to wilt kale. Can be served warm or at room temperature.

Butternut Squash Dumplings   VG   Serves 8

1 butternut squash
½ tsp. salt
¼ tsp. ground pepper
¼ tsp. ground nutmeg
3 - 3½ C. flour
3 T. butter, melted
½ C. shredded Parmesan, Asiago, or Romano cheese

Poke holes all over the squash with a fork or sharp knife. Bake or microwave until tender. Let sit until cool enough to handle, and then cut in half lengthwise. Scoop out and discard the seeds. Flesh should be tender when scraped with a fork. If it is not, return to oven or microwave until tenderness is reached. Scrape out flesh and mash until smooth.

In a large bowl, thoroughly combine 2 cups mashed squash (save any extra for another use) with the salt, pepper, and nutmeg. Stir in flour, 1 cup at a time, until dough forms - it will pull away from inside of the bowl. Turn dough out onto a generously floured work surface. With well-floured hands, knead dough 10 to 12 times. Divide dough in half and cover 1 batch with plastic wrap. Roll the other batch into a ¾-inch thick rope and cut into ½-inch long pieces. Put pieces on a floured baking sheet and set aside. Repeat with remaining dough.

Bring a large pot of salted water to a boil. Drop in the dumplings and boil until they rise to the surface, about 4 minutes. Cook 30 seconds longer and then lift out with a slotted spoon, making sure the water drains from the dumplings. Place in a serving bowl. Gently toss with butter and top with cheese and a sprinkling of ground pepper. Serve hot!

Squash Dinner Rolls **VG**

1½ C. warm milk (105°)
1 (¼-oz.) pkg. active dry yeast
2 T. sugar
1 T. salt
1 egg, lightly beaten
¾ C. cooked & puréed butternut squash (canned pumpkin can be substituted)
5 T. vegetable shortening
4 - 5 C. flour
2 T. butter, melted
2 tsp. poppy or sesame seeds

Combine milk with yeast, sugar, and salt; let stand 5 minutes, then add the egg and beat well to combine. Add squash and shortening. Mash with a fork until the shortening is in small pieces. Add 1½ cups flour and mix well with a wooden spoon. Gradually add flour by the cupful until dough collects around the spoon and pulls away from the sides of the bowl. Transfer dough to a lightly floured work surface and knead for 2 minutes. Put dough in a greased bowl; cover with a towel and let rise in a warm place until doubled in size, about 1-1½ hours. Punch dough down and turn out onto a lightly floured work surface. Knead dough until smooth and supple, about 7 minutes. Cut dough into 4 even pieces; cut each of these into 6 pieces. Roll each piece of dough into a round and arrange rolls on a well-greased baking sheet so they barely touch. Brush with melted butter and sprinkle with poppy or sesame seeds. Cover with plastic wrap and let rise 30 minutes. Bake in a preheated 400° oven until golden brown, about 20 minutes. Let cool, then pull apart to serve.

Creamy Pumpkin Risotto **VG** **GF**   Serves 6

1 small to medium sized pumpkin (cooking variety, not Jack-o-Lantern)
1 C. risotto rice (Arborio)
1 C. white wine (optional)
2 medium onions
1½ T. butter
2 T. olive oil
Minced fresh tarragon or dry fennel seeds, to taste
1 C. Parmesan cheese
6 - 8 C. chicken or vegetable stock (see Bulb, Roots & Tubers chapter for recipe)

To roast pumpkin: using a fork, puncture the squash in several places to allow steam to escape during roasting. Place the whole squash on a cookie sheet and roast at 400° for about an hour, or until the inner flesh is completely soft. Remove from oven and allow to cool. Cut in half and remove seeds and strings. Scoop all the flesh into a bowl. Purée the flesh in a food processor or food mill, reserving 1½ to 2 cups of the puréed pumpkin for the risotto. Use the remaining purée in other recipes such as muffins or pie; it can also be frozen for use later.

To make risotto: heat the stock to simmering. Heat the olive oil in a separate, large saucepan; cook the onions over medium heat until translucent, but not browned. Once onions are soft, add the rice and stir and cook over high heat until the rice is coated and toasted a bit. Now begin adding the hot stock, one ladleful at a time, stirring until the liquid is completely absorbed. After the second ladle of stock is absorbed, add the wine and let it absorb. If not using wine, simply continue with the stock. After the wine and third ladle of stock, stir in the pumpkin purée and tarragon or fennel seeds. Stir until the liquid from the pumpkin is absorbed, then continue with the stock until the rice is soft, but not mushy. Once the rice has reached the perfect creaminess, remove from heat and stir in butter and Parmesan cheese. Serve in shallow soup or pasta style bowls. Garnish with a sprinkling of chopped pecans, roasted pumpkin seeds (see recipe in the *Fruits, Nuts and Seeds* chapter of this book) or peppery nasturtium blossoms that may still be surviving in the garden.

ⓘ**Tip:** save pumpkin seeds to roast for a delicious, nutritious treat.

ⓘ**Fact:** pumpkins are believed to have originated in North America. Seeds from related plants have been found in Mexico dating back to 7000 to 5500 B.C.

ⓘ**Fact:** in the United States, the carved pumpkin was first associated with the harvest season in general, long before it became a symbol of Halloween.

ⓘ**Information:** pumpkin seeds are a good source of vitamin E, iron, magnesium, potassium, zinc, and omega-6 and omega-3 fatty acids.

Pumpkin Caraway Soup QE VG GF

Serves 8 or 10

2 T. olive oil
1 medium onion, chopped
½ tsp. smoky paprika
1 large carrot, peeled and thinly sliced
2 C. pumpkin, peeled and cubed
¼ tsp. whole caraway seeds
1½ C. vegetable stock (see Bulb, Roots & Tubers chapter for recipe)
3 C. milk

In a large saucepan or soup pot, heat oil over medium heat. Add onion, carrots, pumpkin and caraway seeds and sauté, stirring occasionally, for 8-10 minutes, until pumpkin becomes tender and begins to brown (some may stick to the pan). Add stock and simmer 20 minutes. Remove from heat and stir in 2 cups milk. Purée in batches in a blender until smooth, adjusting consistency with remaining milk. Season to taste with salt and pepper. Serve in soup bowls. Sprinkle paprika on top.

Tip: butternut or acorn squash substitute well for the pumpkin in this recipe.

Pumpkin Bread QE VG DF   Makes 1 loaf

2 C. boiled and mashed pumpkin (butternut squash can also be used)
1 C. sugar
1 C. brown sugar
½ C. cooking oil
1 egg
2½ C. flour
½ tsp. salt
½ tsp. cinnamon
½ tsp. cloves
¼ tsp. nutmeg
2 tsp. baking powder
1 C. chopped walnuts

Combine pumpkin, sugar, oil, and egg. Mix well. Combine dry ingredients and add to pumpkin mixture. Stir in nuts. Bake in greased loaf pan at 350° for 1 hour. Test by inserting a toothpick in the center of the loaf. When the toothpick comes out clean, the bread is done.

Zucchini Hummus QE VG GF DF   Serves 8

2 medium zucchini, cut in pieces
¾ C. raw tahini (available in ethnic or food co-op stores)
½ C. fresh lemon juice
¼ C. olive oil
4 cloves garlic
2½ tsp. sea salt
½ T. cumin

Place all ingredients in food processor and blend until smooth.

*ⓘ***Fact:** zucchini was first grown in Mexico around 7,000 years ago, where it was a staple in the diet of indigenous people. European explorers brought the zucchini back to France, Italy, and Great Britain, where it was incorporated into many dishes.

Zucchini "Vichyssoise" QE VG GF   Serves 6

4 - 8 leeks, chopped to make 5 cups - use both white and green parts
8 small white potatoes, chopped to make 4 cups
2 zucchini, chopped to make 3 cups
6 C. chicken stock (or vegetable broth for vegetarian version)
1 T. unsalted butter
1 T. olive oil
1 tsp. sea salt
½ tsp. fresh ground pepper
2 T. cream
Fresh chives for garnish

Heat butter and oil in a large soup pot. Add leeks and sauté over medium-low heat for 5 minutes. Add potatoes, zucchini, chicken stock, salt, and pepper and bring to a boil. Lower heat and simmer 30 minutes. Cool awhile, then blend using an immersion blender or work in batches using a regular blender. Add cream and season to taste. Serve hot or cold, garnished with chopped chives.

Zucchini "Lasagna" VG GF   Serves 8

3 C. tomato sauce
4 large zucchini, sliced lengthwise very thin, about ⅛-inch thick
Salt and freshly ground pepper
1 lb. Ricotta cheese
1 lb. Provolone, Fontina or Mozzarella cheese, shredded
2 C. sautéed onions and mushrooms

Heat oven to 350°. Spread 1 cup sauce on bottom of a 9"x13" pan. Arrange an overlapping layer of zucchini slices in the pan. Using half the ricotta, distribute it by teaspoonfuls evenly over the zucchini layer. Layer on 1/3 of the shredded cheese and half the sautéed vegetables. Arrange another layer of zucchini and repeat fillings using remaining ricotta, vegetables, and another third of the cheese. Add final layer of zucchini on top. Spread with 2 more cups of tomato sauce. Sprinkle top with remaining cheese. Bake for 1 hour until casserole is bubbly and cheese is lightly browned.

ⓘ **Tip:** this recipe is best made a day in advance, refrigerated, and cut cold into serving portions before re-warming to serve. Warm in oven or microwave until hot.

ⓘ **Tip:** try replacing half the zucchini with an equal portion of thinly sliced eggplant; lightly dust slices with salt on one side.

ⓘ **Information**: zucchini contains protein, fiber, vitamins A, C, K and B, and minerals such as phosphorous, copper, manganese magnesium and potassium.

Chilled Zucchini Soup with Cilantro Cream   VG GF   Serves 4 to 6

1 T. olive oil
2 C. sliced onion (about 1 medium onion)
6 medium zucchini, cut into ¼-inch rounds
4 C. chicken broth (or vegetable broth for vegetarian version)
4 T. fresh chopped cilantro, divided in half
½ C. sour cream
3 cloves garlic, minced
Cilantro sprigs for garnish

Heat oil in a heavy pot over medium heat. Add onion and sauté until tender, about 8 minutes. Add two-thirds of the garlic and stir for 1 minute. Add zucchini; stir to coat. Stir in broth; bring to a boil. Cover, reduce heat to a simmer, and cook until zucchini is tender, about 10 minutes. Cool to lukewarm. Add half the chopped cilantro. Purée the soup using an immersion blender <u>or</u> working in batches, purée in a blender or food processor until smooth. Transfer to a large bowl, season to taste with salt and pepper. Cover and chill until cold, about 4 hours. Can be made a day ahead if kept chilled. Serve with a dollop of cilantro cream made by whisking together the sour cream, remaining cilantro, remaining minced garlic, and salt and pepper to taste. Cilantro cream may also be made one day ahead.

ⓘ **Tip:** this soup is also good served hot. Vary it by topping the soup with a few medium-sized cooked shrimp that have been marinated in a lemon juice-olive oil dressing.

ⓘ **Tip:** zucchini are best when less than eight inches in length, when the seeds are still soft and immature.

Sautéed Zucchini and Tomatoes QE VG GF DF   Serves 6

2 T. olive oil
1½ lbs. zucchini, cut in ½ -inch slices
2 large cloves garlic, sliced
1½ tsp. chopped fresh rosemary
2 C. small cherry tomatoes, halved
1/3 C. halved, pitted Kalamata olives
¼ C. thinly sliced fresh basil
1 T. balsamic vinegar

Heat oil in a large skillet over medium-high heat. Add zucchini, garlic, and rosemary. Sprinkle with salt and pepper and sauté until zucchini is just tender, about 5 minutes. Add tomatoes and olives; sauté until tomatoes just begin to soften, about 2 minutes. Mix in the basil and vinegar. Season to taste with salt and pepper.

Zucchini - Corn Casserole QE VG GF   Serves 4 or 6

3 C. sliced zucchini, cut ¼-inch thick
2 C. corn, cut from the cob
1 small jalapeño pepper, finely diced or 1 (4-oz.) can diced green chilies
1½ C. shredded sharp cheddar cheese
2 eggs
½ tsp. salt
½ tsp. garlic powder

Steam zucchini slices over water until tender when pierced, about 4 minutes. Drain, then combine with corn, chilies, and one cup of cheese. Set aside.

Beat eggs with salt and garlic powder. Stir into vegetable mixture. Turn into a greased, shallow, 1½-qt. casserole. Sprinkle with remaining half cup cheese. Bake uncovered for 20 minutes in a 350° oven. The liquid in the dish should appear set and cheese melted.

ⓘTip: zucchini blossoms are considered an edible delicacy. Pick blossoms during morning hours when they are fresh and soft. To prepare, open blossoms and carefully inspect for insects. Pull off any calyces (outer green portion that encloses the flower) attached firmly at the base. Enjoy raw or cooked. Often served stuffed and deep-fried.

Sautéed Zucchini and Carrot Ribbons QE VG GF DF Serves 4 or 6

1½ lbs. zucchini
2 - 3 large carrots
2 T. olive oil
¼ C. fresh tarragon leaves
Salt and pepper to taste

Using a peeler (like you are peeling potatoes), peel in a lengthwise direction several slices (ribbons) of zucchini. Do the same with the carrots. Heat the oil in a large skillet over medium-high heat. Add the zucchini and carrot ribbons to the pan and sauté, tossing occasionally, about 5 minutes. Once tender-crisp, add the tarragon leaves and toss again to blend all the flavors. Season with salt and pepper to taste and serve at once.

Zucchini Cakes QE VG Serves 6

1 lb. zucchini, coarsely grated (use a food processor if available)
1 tsp. salt
4 T. flour
2 T. finely grated Parmesan cheese
2 T. minced green onion
1 large egg, beaten
½ tsp. fresh ground pepper
Canola oil (for frying)
Sour cream or unflavored yogurt and fresh dill or fennel fronds for serving

Place grated zucchini in a colander set over a bowl. Sprinkle with salt and place a plate on top of the zucchini to weigh it down. Let stand for 30 minutes to release water content and drain. Squeeze zucchini dry using paper towels, then transfer to a bowl. Add flour, Parmesan, green onion, beaten egg, and pepper; stir. Coat a large non-stick skillet with enough oil to coat, then heat to medium-high. Working in batches, drop 1/4 cupfuls (use the 1/4 measuring cup) of zucchini mixture into skillet. Flatten the cakes into rounds with a spatula. Cook until golden, about 1 to 1½ minutes per side. Transfer to a baking sheet and keep warm in a 325° oven until all cakes are cooked and ready to serve. Place the cakes on a platter to serve. Top each cake with a dollop of sour cream or yogurt and a sprinkling of fresh dill or fennel fronds.

Summer Vegetable Pasta QE   Serves 4

8 oz. pasta such as rotini or cavatappi
4 slices bacon, chopped
2 tsp. olive oil
1 C. chopped onion
1 tsp. minced garlic
1 medium zucchini, quartered lengthwise and cut into ¼-inch thick slices
1 C. fresh corn kernels (about 2 ears)
1 pint grape tomatoes
½ C. shaved Parmesan cheese, divided
¼ C. small fresh basil leaves
½ tsp. salt
¼ tsp. black pepper

Cook pasta according to package directions; drain and set aside. While pasta cooks, cook bacon in a large skillet over medium-high heat until crisp. Remove bacon from the pan with a slotted spoon, reserving drippings in the pan. Add oil to drippings, followed by the onion and garlic. Sauté 2 minutes, stirring occasionally. Add zucchini; cook 3 minutes, stirring occasionally. Stir in corn and tomatoes; cook 5 minutes or until tomatoes burst, stirring occasionally. Add pasta to tomato mixture; toss and cook 1 minute or until thoroughly heated, stirring frequently. Remove from heat. Add 1/4 cup cheese, basil, salt, and pepper; toss to combine. Sprinkle with remaining cheese and serve.

Garden Vegetable Minestrone Soup VG   Serves 6 to 8

6 C. any type broth (use vegetable stock for vegetarian version)
1 onion, roughly chopped
2 - 3 carrots, sliced on the diagonal
4 large fresh tomatoes, roughly chopped or 1 (16-oz) can diced tomatoes, undrained
4 oz. uncooked spaghetti, broken into 1-inch pieces
2 medium zucchini, sliced
1 (16-oz.) can kidney beans, drained
1 C. shredded cabbage
¼ C. fresh chopped basil
¼ tsp. freshly ground pepper
1 tsp. salt
Grated Romano or Parmesan cheese for serving

Pour broth into soup pot. Add onion, carrots, and tomatoes to the broth. Cover and heat until carrots begin to soften. Add the spaghetti, zucchini, kidney beans, and cabbage; simmer until carrots and cabbage are cooked all the way through. Stir in basil, salt, and pepper. Heat for another minute, stirring to blend the flavors. Cover and let stand for several minutes. Ladle into soup bowls and top with grated cheese to serve.

Zucchini & Carrot Casserole QE VG DF   Serves 4 to 6

1 C. baking mix (like Bisquick)
3 eggs
½ C. vegetable oil
1 C. shredded carrots
1 C. shredded cheddar cheese
3 C. shredded zucchini
1 small onion, chopped
Salt and pepper to taste

Preheat oven to 350°. Grease an 8 x 8-inch baking pan. In a large bowl, combine all the ingredients, then pour into the baking pan. Bake 35 to 45 minutes.

Zucchini Bread VG DF

Makes 2 loaves

3 eggs
1 C. cooking oil
2 C. sugar
2 C. unpeeled, grated zucchini
3 T. vanilla
3 C. flour
1 tsp. salt
1 tsp. soda
1 tsp. baking powder
3 tsp. cinnamon
1 C. walnuts, roughly chopped

Beat eggs until foamy. Gradually beat in sugar, oil, and vanilla. Stir in zucchini. Sift together dry ingredients and add to zucchini mixture. Add nuts and stir until blended in. Be careful not to over stir. Pour batter into two greased and papered loaf pans. Bake at 325° for one hour or until a toothpick inserted near center comes out clean. Cool in pans for about ten minutes, before removing. Complete cooling on a cooling rack.

Fruiting Vegetables

Basic Ways of Cooking & Serving

Vegetable	Preparation	Cooking Time	Ways to Serve
Artichokes	Cut off 1 inch of the top with sharp knife. Trim stem leaving ½ inch stub. Remove outer lower leaves and thorny leaf tips.	Boil 20-45 minutes or until leaf pulls easily away.	Place upright on plate. Offer melted butter mixed with a little lemon juice; mayonnaise mixed with lemon juice and prepared mustard; also sour cream dip.
Eggplant	Paring not necessary. Leave whole or cut into strips or slices 1 inch thick.	Sauté 5-10 minutes in butter or drippings.	Buttered with salt, pepper, Parmesan, minced chives or parsley. Vary with a few peppercorns, parsley, green onions, crushed garlic, or bay leaf. Fried, stuffed, scalloped.
Cucumber	Cucumber is sensitive to changes in temperature. Will keep for 3-5 days in the refrigerator. Skin may be left on for recipes, especially if very fresh and not too large.		Grated or cut lengthwise, sliced or diced, raw cucumber can be used with vinaigrette, yogurt, or sour cream, or stuffed with seafood. It is also served as salad and makes a good soup. Can be preserved, marinated, or cooked. When cooked, it is prepared in same way as zucchini, which it can replace in most recipes.
Peppers	Remove stem, seeds, and membrane. Leave whole to stuff and bake. Chop or cut in slivers or rings to use as an ingredient.	Parboil whole 5 minutes, bake at 350° for 25-30 minutes. Sauté pieces 5 minutes to use as ingredient.	Whole - stuffed and baked. Used as an ingredient in casseroles, scrambles or stir-fries.
Tomatoes	Peel if desired. Leave whole or cut in quarters or slices.	To cook, cover pan, add no water, season with bay leaf or other herbs, if desired. Bring to boil, then simmer 8-10 minutes. Broil 3-5 minutes.	Vary with fennel, basil, oregano, sage, tarragon, or marjoram.

Tip: don't cut eggplant until ready to use as it discolors.

Tip: to easily peel tomatoes for cooking or slicing, cut an X in the bottom, drop into simmering water until skin loosens, then peel off with fingers.

Tip: do not use aluminum pans when cooking tomatoes. The acid reacts with the aluminum causing tomatoes to fade in color and become more bitter. The acid in tomatoes can also pit and discolor aluminum cookware.

Tip: wear gloves when handling jalapeño and other hot peppers, to keep the heat producing acids from getting on your hands and in your eyes, if rubbed.

Now Add Some Creativity!

Cucumber Salad `QE` `VG` `GF` `DF`   Serves 6 to 8

6 C. sliced cucumbers (leave peel on if fresh and not tough)
1 C. thinly sliced radishes
½ C. chopped bell pepper
¼ C. flat-leaf parsley, roughly chopped
1 tsp. finely grated lemon rind
2 T. fresh lemon juice
1 T. olive oil
1½ tsp. white wine vinegar
½ tsp. salt
¼ tsp. pepper

Combine cucumber, radishes, bell pepper, and parsley in a bowl. Whisk remaining ingredients together and pour over the cucumber mixture. Toss well to coat. Serve at room temperature or chilled.

Creamy Cucumber Salad `QE` `VG` `GF`   Serves 6

2 large cucumbers, thinly sliced lengthwise
2½ C. thinly sliced red onion
¼ C. plain yogurt
2 T. chopped fresh dill
1 T. chopped fresh parsley
1½ tsp. chopped mint
2 T. freshly squeezed lemon juice
1 T. olive oil
2 tsp. Dijon mustard
¼ tsp. each sugar, salt and pepper
1 clove garlic

Place sliced cucumber and onion in a large bowl. Place remaining ingredients in a food processor and process until well blended. Pour mixture over the cucumber and onions. Toss to coat and serve.

Tomato and Bread Salad ~ Panzanella   QE VG DF   Serves 4

2 C. diced ripe tomatoes, any variety or color
¼ C. finely chopped red onion
½ tsp. salt
1½ T. olive oil
2 tsp. lemon juice
2 C. day-old country style bread, cut into ½ -inch cubes and dried
¼ C. roughly chopped flat-leafed parsley
Pepper to taste

Combine tomatoes, onion, salt, olive oil, and lemon juice. Toss gently with dried bread cubes and parsley. Season with freshly ground black pepper.

Tip: to dry bread cubes, air-dry overnight or bake for 20 minutes at 325°.

Nana's Tomato Salad   QE VG GF DF   Serves 4

2 - 3 large ripe tomatoes
Small bunch of basil leaves, cut into chiffonade
2 T. olive oil
1 garlic clove pressed
Salt to taste
Splash of water

Mix all ingredients and serve with good quality bread. In my family, the bread MUST be dunked in the tomato salad.

Note: to make chiffonade, stack and roll basil leaves and cut in thin ribbons.

Tip: if you've got a great vine-ripened tomato, don't kill its flavor by storing it in the refrigerator.

Tip: put unripe tomatoes in a brown bag and leave them at room temperature until they ripen, usually in a day or two.

Fact: 93% of American gardening households grow tomatoes.

Crusty Broiled Tomatoes QE VG DF   Serves 2

2 ripe tomatoes
¼ C. dried bread crumbs
1 T. olive oil
1 clove garlic, minced
Salt and pepper to taste

Preheat oven to 350°. Cut tomatoes in half horizontally and gently squeeze out the seeds. Drain the halves cut side down, then pat dry. Combine remaining ingredients and spoon onto the cut side of the tomatoes. Arrange in a baking dish and bake for 15 minutes, then place under broiler just until tops are browned and crusty.

Oven-Dried Tomatoes VG GF DF

20 Roma tomatoes, firm-ripe
4 cloves garlic, halved
4 T. olive oil
2 T. balsamic vinegar
2 T. finely chopped herb of choice (basil, flat-leaf parsley, rosemary)
Sea salt
Freshly ground pepper

Trim stem ends from tomatoes and quarter lengthwise. Remove seeds. Place in a large, nonmetallic bowl and add the olive oil, vinegar, and herbs; mix well. Season to taste with salt and pepper. Cover bowl and allow to marinate in refrigerator for 2 to 3 hours.

Preheat oven to 200°. Place tomatoes in a single layer on a nonstick baking sheet. Bake 16 to 20 hours. Cool before storing. To store, place dried tomatoes in sterilized glass jars and pour olive oil over to cover. Seal tightly with lids. Store in the refrigerator for 2 to 3 weeks, or place in a zipper-style bag and freeze for up to 3 months. Use in sauces or as an appetizer ingredient.

ⓘ **Tip:** the best time to place the tomatoes in the oven for drying is around 7:00 in the evening and then bake them throughout the night. The next morning you'll have plump, juicy, and intensely flavorful tomatoes.

Roasted Tomatoes QE VG GF DF   Serves 4 to 5

12 Roma or plum type tomatoes, halved lengthwise, cored and seeded
4 T. olive oil
1½ T. balsamic vinegar
2 cloves garlic, minced
2 tsp. sugar
1½ tsp. sea salt
½ tsp. freshly ground pepper

Preheat oven to 450°. Arrange tomato halves on a baking sheet, cut side up. Drizzle tomatoes with the oil and balsamic vinegar, then sprinkle with garlic, sugar, salt, and pepper. Roast until tomatoes are beginning to caramelize, about 25 to 30 minutes. Serve warm or at room temperature.

ⓘ **Fact:** the tomato is America's fourth most popular fresh-market vegetable behind potatoes, lettuce , and onions.

Tomato and Olive Bruschetta QE VG DF   Makes 8 servings

4 slices rustic bread, each slice cut in half
½ C. olive oil
2 cl. garlic, minced
3 ripe tomatoes, roughly chopped
½ tsp. salt
¼ tsp. pepper
½ C. olives (green or black or both), chopped
¼ C. flat-leaf parsley, roughly chopped
Juice of 1 lemon

Combine olive oil and garlic. Brush on both sides of bread slices. Broil bread until brown on both sides.

Toss chopped tomatoes with 1 tablespoon of the garlic-oil mixture, salt, pepper, olives, and parsley. Season to taste with lemon juice. Top each piece of grilled bread with a small amount of tomato-olive mixture. Arrange on a plate and serve.

Fresh Tomato Pasta VG   Serves 6

3 lbs. fresh tomatoes cut into bite size pieces
Coarse salt
Red pepper flakes
1 - 2 sliced garlic cloves
Freshly ground black pepper
1 lb. cooked spaghetti, hot
2 C. saved pasta cooking water
½ lb. crumbled goat cheese
1 C. torn fresh basil or Italian parsley
Balsamic or sherry vinegar
Homemade croutons in bite size pieces (DO NOT use store bought!)

Put tomatoes, garlic, salt, red pepper flakes to taste, 2 tablespoons vinegar, and approximately 1/3 cup oil, depending on juiciness of tomatoes. Let macerate (stand to become soft & syrupy) for 1 hour. Remove the garlic slices, if desired. Cook spaghetti in well salted boiling water until al dente. Drain & toss with sauce. Moisten sauce with reserved pasta cooking water for desired consistency. Add cheese and basil and check for seasoning. Top with homemade croutons (recipe follows).

Homemade Croutons QE VG DF

Day-old French bread
Olive oil
Salt
Freshly ground black pepper
¼ tsp. red pepper flakes

Preheat oven to 400°. Cut bread into cubes and place in a large bowl. Drizzle cubes with olive oil, salt, pepper and red pepper flakes. Mix well. Spread seasoned bread cubes onto a baking sheet and bake for about 15 minutes.

Fresh Tomato Salsa QE VG GF DF   Makes about 1½ cups

½ C. cilantro leaves, chopped
1 C. chopped tomatoes
¼ C. diced red bell pepper
¼ C. diced red onion

1 small jalapeño pepper, seeded and minced
2 T. freshly squeezed lime juice

Thoroughly combine all ingredients. Cover and refrigerate until ready to use.

Pasta Amatriciana　QE　　　　　　　　　　　　　　　　Serves 6

¼ lb. pancetta
2 onions, chopped
½ red pepper, chopped
2 lbs. fresh tomatoes roasted in oven for 40 minutes or one (28 oz.) can fire roasted diced tomatoes
Olive oil
Red pepper flakes to taste
2 T. vermouth
2 t. balsamic vinegar
Salt and black pepper to taste
1 lb. cooked penne or any short pasta of choice
¼ C. chopped parsley for garnish
Romano cheese for serving

Sauté pancetta until crisp in large heavy pan. Remove pancetta and save the drippings. Add 2 to 3 tablespoons olive oil to the drippings and slowly cook onions and red pepper until caramelized. Deglaze pan with vermouth. Add tomatoes, cover, and simmer for 20 minutes. Taste for seasoning and add pancetta and vinegar. Toss the sauce with the hot cooked pasta and parsley. Serve with grated Romano.

Tip: if you don't have vermouth for de-glazing, simply add vegetable or chicken stock, white wine, clear soda, fruit juice, or plain water. You can be as conservative or creative as you like.

Information: pancetta is an Italian type of dry cured meat that is similar to bacon. If all else fails and you cannot find pancetta, prosciutto or American-style bacon can be used as a substitute in recipes. When using prosciutto as a substitute for pancetta, only lightly cook it.

Mediterranean Chopped Salad   QE VG GF   Serves 4

2 fresh tomatoes, seeded and chopped
2 green onions, chopped
1 yellow pepper, seeded and chopped
1 cucumber peeled, seeded and chopped
3 T. black Kalamata or other oil-cured olives, pitted and chopped
2 T. fresh parsley or mint, chopped
3 T. fresh-squeezed lemon juice
2 T. olive oil
Salt and pepper to taste
¼ C. feta cheese, crumbled (optional)

Whisk together the lemon juice and oil in a serving bowl. Add remaining ingredients, except salt and pepper, and stir to combine. Season to taste with salt and pepper. Chill awhile before serving so the flavors can mingle.

Tomato Lentil Salad   QE VG GF DF   Serves 4 to 6

3 C. cooked brown or green lentils
2 T. shallots, chopped
½ red or yellow pepper, chopped
1 C. parsley or cilantro, chopped
½ C. peeled and seeded cucumber, diced
2 C. grape or cherry tomatoes, halved if large
½ C. olive oil
1 T. Dijon mustard
2 - 3 T. fresh lemon juice, to taste
1 T. lemon zest
1 tsp. cumin
1 tsp. paprika
Salt and pepper to taste
Lemon wedges for serving

Mix lentils, shallots, pepper, parsley or cilantro, cucumber and tomatoes in large bowl. Shake rest of ingredients (except lemon wedges) in a large jar until blended. Pour half of dressing in bowl and keep adding until salad is moist. Correct seasonings. Serve with lemon wedges.

Easy Gazpacho   QE VG GF DF   Serves 6

6 very ripe tomatoes, peeled and chopped
1 medium cucumber peeled and finely chopped
1 small onion, finely chopped
1 green pepper, finely chopped
1 small clove garlic, minced
1½ - 2½ C. tomato juice
¼ C. olive oil
2 T. wine vinegar
1 tsp. salt
¼ tsp. pepper
Few drops hot sauce (like Tabasco)

In a large bowl, combine all ingredients. Chill until very cold. If desired, an ice cube can be added to each bowl when serving.

Mexicali Rice   QE VG GF DF   Serves 4

1 C. bell pepper (red, orange or green or mixture), chopped
½ small jalapeño pepper, minced
1 tomato or tomatillo, chopped
1 - 2 T. fresh cilantro, roughly chopped
½ tsp. finely shredded lime peel
1 tsp. lime juice
2 C. vegetable stock (see Bulb, Roots & Tubers chapter for recipe)
⅛ tsp. salt
1 C. basmati rice, white or brown (long-grain may be substituted)
½ tsp. cumin

In a medium saucepan, bring broth and salt to a boil. Add rice and cumin and return to a boil. Reduce heat, cover and simmer 20 minutes or until rice is tender and liquid absorbed. Stir in remaining ingredients and serve.

Avocado, Onion, and Pepper Salad QE VG GF DF   Serves 4

2 ripe avocados, sliced
½ C. sliced red onion or green onions
Juice of 1 lime or lemon
¼ C. finely chopped cilantro or flat-leaf parsley
½ red bell pepper, chopped
2 T. olive oil
½ tsp. sea salt (or other coarse salt)
½ tsp. freshly ground black pepper

Place all ingredients in a bowl. Toss to coat, then serve.

ⓘ **Tip:** for more "heat" substitute 1/2 small jalapeño pepper, thinly sliced, for the red bell pepper.

Confetti Peppers & Corn QE VG GF   Serves 2 to 4

½ C. red pepper, diced
½ C. green pepper, diced
1 jalapeño pepper, seeded and diced
¼ C. red onion, diced
1 - 2 C. fresh corn kernels
2 T. butter
Sour cream or plain yogurt (optional)

Melt 1 tablespoon of the butter in a large skillet. Add corn and stir-fry for 1 minute. Add remaining ingredients and cook until peppers and onion are tender. Serve as is or add about 1/2 cup sour cream or yogurt, stirring constantly until heated through.

Eggplant and Squash Ratatouille VG GF DF   Serves 6

2 T. olive oil
1 large onion, diced
1 small eggplant, diced
2 medium zucchini, diced

2 medium yellow squash, diced
1 bell pepper, diced
1 T. flour
3 tomatoes, seeded and cut into pieces
4 tsp. combination of fresh herbs - oregano, thyme, rosemary, marjoram, savory, lavender or 2 tsp. dried Herbs de Province
1 tsp. salt
Freshly ground black pepper
Fresh basil leaves, chopped (optional)
Grated Parmesan cheese (optional)

Heat olive oil in a heavy bottomed pot or Dutch oven. Add onion and cook until translucent, about 5 minutes. Combine eggplant, zucchini, yellow squash, and green pepper in a large paper bag. Add flour and shake bag to coat vegetables. Add floured vegetables, along with tomatoes, herbs, salt, and pepper to the pot. Reduce heat to simmer, cover pot and cook gently for 1 hour or until all vegetables are tender. To serve, garnish with chopped basil and/or grated Parmesan cheese.

Stacked Eggplant Parmesan VG   Serves 4

2 medium-sized eggplants
Salt
1 C. soft bread crumbs
¼ C. chopped fresh basil (or other fresh herbs from the garden)
¾ C. grated Parmesan cheese
¼ C. olive oil
16 oz. Mozzarella cheese, thinly sliced
2 C. basic tomato sauce (see recipe in Fruiting Vegetables chapter) or use jarred
    chunky style pasta sauce from the store

Preheat oven to 350°. Slice eggplant crosswise into ¼-inch thick slices. Place in a colander, sprinkle with salt and set in sink to drain liquid for at least 30 minutes. Rinse and dry on towels.

Combine bread crumbs, basil, and 1/4 cup of the Parmesan cheese in a flat pan. Heat olive oil in a large skillet. Press the eggplant slices into the bread mixture and sauté in the olive oil until light golden brown on both sides. Repeat with all of the eggplant pieces.

 Using a baking sheet, assemble as follows: Place 4 of the largest eggplant pieces on the pan, top each with 2 tablespoons tomato sauce, then a slice of mozzarella cheese. Sprinkle with Parmesan, then repeat the layering process until all the ingredients have been used, making sure to finish with the Parmesan. Place in the preheated oven and bake until the top of each eggplant stack is golden brown and bubbly, about 15 to 20 minutes.

Artichoke Linguine   QE VG   Serves 6

½ C. olive oil
¼ C. flour
1 C. chicken broth (use vegetable stock for vegetarian version)
1 clove garlic, minced
2 - 3 T. fresh lemon juice
1 T. lemon zest
3 steamed trimmed artichokes, or 1 (14 oz.) can artichokes (not marinated),
    chopped into bite size pieces

2 T. parsley, chopped
Hot smoked paprika or Tabasco to taste
Salt and pepper to taste
1 lb. cooked linguine
Parmesan cheese

Heat olive oil and add flour, stirring constantly until mixture is a light brown. Stir in garlic, paprika, or Tabasco and add broth. Cook 3 minutes. Add artichokes, cook 3 minutes. Add lemon juice, zest, parsley and correct seasonings. Toss with hot pasta and about 1/4 cup Parmesan. Serve with grated Parmesan.

White Bean Stew VG GF DF   Serves 6

2¼ C. small white dried beans, such as Navy beans
1 - 2 carrots, cut into chunks
1 medium onion, cut into chunks
A few celery leaves
2 cloves garlic
2 - 3 medium tomatoes, peeled and cut into chunks
2 sprigs rosemary
1 bay leaf
Freshly ground pepper
Sea salt
Olive oil

Soak beans covered in water overnight. Drain; put in a soup pot with the rest of the ingredients except salt and oil. Cover with water and simmer for 1 hour or until beans and vegetables are tender, adding salt to taste toward the end. To serve as soup, do not drain. To serve as stew, drain most of the water. Serve with a drizzle of oil.

ⓘ**Tip:** if you have an abundance of green beans in the garden, dry the small white beans inside, as described in the Legumes and Grains chapter.

ⓘ**Information:** dried beans and other legumes are full of nutrients, including fiber, protein, complex carbohydrates, minerals, and vitamins.

Vegetable Chili QE VG GF DF   Serves 8

1 large onion, chopped
1 red pepper, seeded and diced
1 jalapeño, seeded with ribs removed, minced
2 ribs celery, diced
2 - 3 carrots, diced
1 - 2 cloves minced garlic
2 medium zucchini, diced
1 (28 oz.) can diced fired roasted tomatoes
3 T. tomato paste
1 (28 oz.) can hominy
4 C. cooked red or pinto beans
1 quart vegetable or chicken broth (may not use all of it)
1/3 C. approximately of chili powder (try an ancho blend)
2 T. ground cumin
2 T. Mexican oregano
2 T. dark cocoa powder
2 T. vermouth or vodka
Salt and black pepper to taste
Apple cider vinegar to taste

Sauté onion, carrots, celery, and pepper in large pot until golden. Add garlic for 30 seconds. Add cumin and chili powder and cook for 30 seconds. Add tomato paste and cook for 30 seconds. Add vermouth or vodka to de-glaze the pan. Add tomatoes, zucchini, and broth. Simmer for about 40 minutes. Add beans, hominy, and oregano. Add some water, if too dry. Cook for 10 to 15 minutes. Check for seasonings and add splash of vinegar at end. Serve with condiments of lime wedges, sliced radishes, sour cream or crema, shredded Cheddar or Mexican cheese, and steamed rice. Also good made with 2 lbs. of ground turkey, beef or pork.

Tip: fire-roasted tomatoes add a delicious, smoky flavor to chili, salsas, and pasta sauce. You can purchase canned fire-roasted tomatoes at the store, but it is easy to roast tomatoes on a gas or charcoal grill.

Tex-Mex Tortilla Soup QE GF

Serves 6 to 8

2 T. olive oil
1 C. chopped onion
3 cloves garlic, minced
½ large red bell pepper, chopped
½ green bell pepper, chopped
1 jalapeño pepper, minced
1 T. chili powder
1½ tsp. crushed red pepper
½ tsp. salt
½ tsp. cumin
½ tsp. freshly ground black pepper
3 C. cooked shredded chicken
2 C. corn kernels (fresh or frozen)
1 qt. low-sodium chicken broth
2 large tomatoes or 1 (15-oz.) can diced tomatoes
1 (15-oz.) can black beans, rinsed and drained
¼ C. chopped fresh cilantro
Crumbled Queso Fresco cheese, for serving
Crisp corn tortilla chips, for serving

> *This soup is spicy and hot. You may want to cut back on the jalapeño, chili powder, and crushed red pepper, if a milder soup is to your liking. I also like fire-roasted canned tomatoes, if I don't have fresh tomatoes to use.*
> *- Jennifer Grant*

In a soup pot, heat the oil. Add the onion, garlic, and peppers. Sauté for 3 minutes. Add chili powder, crushed red pepper, salt, cumin, and black pepper. Sauté for 30 seconds, then add the chicken, corn, broth, tomatoes, and beans. Bring to a boil, cover, reduce heat, and simmer for 5 or 6 minutes. Ladle soup into bowls and top with Queso Fresco and tortilla chips.

ⓘInformation: Queso Fresco is a traditional Mexican cheese widely used in a variety of dishes. Firm-textured, this fresh white cheese is slightly salty, with a mild, tangy taste similar to farmer's cheese.

ⓘTip: to make your own tortilla chips, spray tortillas with cooking spray, sprinkle with salt and/or seasonings of your choice, then cut corn or flour tortillas into wedges and place in a single layer on a baking sheet. Bake at 350° for 5 minutes, until crisp and lightly browned or broil for 5 minutes.

Basic Fresh Tomato Sauce QE VG GF DF   Makes about 1 quart sauce

4 lbs. tomatoes, preferably Roma plum but any variety will do
2 T. olive oil
1 large onion, roughly chopped
5 cloves garlic, chopped (about 2 T.)
1 tsp. sugar
2 T. tomato paste
1 C. fresh basil leaves, stems removed
Salt and freshly ground pepper

Cut tomatoes in half and squeeze out as many seeds as you can. Dice tomatoes. Heat olive oil in a large saucepan or Dutch oven. Add onions and cook until soft and beginning to turn brown, about 10 minutes. Stir in the garlic, sugar, and tomato paste; cook 2 minutes more, stirring constantly. Add tomatoes; cook 10 minutes until mixture becomes brothy.

Uncover, lower heat to a slow simmer and cook 30 minutes more until all tomatoes are fully softened; season to taste. If you prefer chunky sauce, add the basil, if desired. For smooth sauce, purée and strain, then add basil at the end.

> *I have used this recipe for years. It is a great way to use tomatoes when your harvest is extra bountiful. I often alter the recipe with different or additional herbs and sometimes add a variety of Italian olives if I'm making Pasta Puttanesca. In a "good tomato" year, I make lots of this sauce and package it up in freezer bags so we can enjoy it all winter long.*
>
> *- Jennifer Grant*

Tip: be sure to use a pan that is non-reactive (stainless steel, enamel or glass-lined); copper and aluminum reacts with acidic foods like tomatoes, altering flavor and color.

Easy Tomato Sauce QE VG GF DF   Serves 4

1 T. cold-pressed, virgin coconut oil
½ red onion, chopped
3 stalks celery, chopped
2 carrots, peeled

5 large tomatoes, blanched
2 - 4 cloves garlic, minced
2 C. water
Fine ground sea salt and freshly ground black pepper, to taste
Optional herbs - fresh basil, parsley, and/or oregano

Chop all the vegetables and put them in a large stock pot that has been coated with coconut oil. Cook over medium heat, stirring often. After 15 minutes, add the garlic and cook another 5 minutes until browned. In the meantime, blanch the tomatoes in a large saucepan of boiling water. Remove tomatoes from the water, peel, and add to the vegetables, along with 2 cups water. If using herbs, add to the sauce at this time and simmer together for about 10 minutes. Transfer cooked sauce to a blender and mix until thoroughly puréed, then transfer back to the stock pot. Season with salt and pepper to taste. Keep warm if you are going to use right away or store in an airtight glass container in the refrigerator or freezer.

Make It Yourself Catsup   QE VG GF DF

1½ C. tomatoes (processed in blender or food processor)
3 T. pitted dates
¼ C. olive oil
1 tsp. salt
1 T. apple cider vinegar
½ C. sun-dried tomatoes

Blend (or food process) fresh tomatoes, dates, oil, salt and vinegar until smooth. Add sun-dried tomatoes last and blend until thick and well mixed.

Plum Tomato Chutney   QE VG GF DF

Makes about 3 cups

1/3 C. sugar
1 lemon, juiced
6 ripe red plum tomatoes, seeded and roughly chopped
6 ripe yellow plum tomatoes, seeded and roughly chopped
¼ C. red onion, finely diced
¼ C. fresh cilantro, roughly chopped (optional)

Mix sugar with 1/2 cup water in a saucepan. Cover and cook over high heat until water is evaporated and molten sugar begins to turn golden brown. Pour in lemon juice to stop sugar from cooking and bring it up from the bottom of the pan. Add tomatoes and onion and simmer for no more than 5 minutes, to warm the tomatoes, not cook them. Remove from heat and allow to cool in a colander or large strainer so excess water can drain out. Stir in cilantro.

ⓘ Tip: use this chutney as an accompaniment with fried tofu or add some, along with olive oil and salt (to taste), to cooked quinoa for a healthy, flavorful salad.

"Lime" Sweet Pickles   QE VG GF DF

7 lbs. pickling cucumbers (or enough to fill a 2-gallon crock)
1 C. pickling lime (available where pickling supplies are sold)
1 gallon water
9 rounded cups sugar
2 quarts cider vinegar
1 T. pickling spices
1 tsp. celery seeds
1 tsp. cloves

Scrub the cucumbers, cut crosswise, and place in a 2-gallon crock. Mix lime with the water and add to the cucumbers. Compress with a weight to keep covered. Soak 24 hours and then rinse well to remove <u>all traces</u> (very important) of the lime. Cover with clear water, let set for 3 hours, then drain and rinse well.

> *This recipe has been in my family for several generations. Note that it can be difficult to find "pickling lime." We often substitute agricultural lime since it is chemically identical.*
>
> *- Mike Extine*

Prepare the pickling solution of sugar, vinegar, and salt in a stainless steel pot. Prepare the spice mixture of pickling spices, celery seeds, and cloves in a cheesecloth/muslin bag; add to the pickling solution. Heat until warm/hot and the sugar dissolves.

Cover the drained cucumbers with the heated vinegar solution and let stand 12 to 24 hours. Transfer from the crock to stainless steel pot and bring to a boil. Boil 45 minutes or until the sugar solution penetrates the cucumbers and they are "clear" in appearance. Pack in prepared, sterile jars and seal. Place in a water bath for 15 minutes. Remove from the water bath, cool and store. Pickles will be ready to eat in a few weeks.

ⓘ**Information:** pickling lime is a white powder used in older pickle recipes to add crispness.

ⓘ**Important:** pickling lime must be washed off the cucumbers completely before they are placed in vinegar. Failure to do so can create an environment for bacteria such as botulinum to thrive.

ⓘ**Information:** there are many types of pickles: fresh pack (or quick process) pickles, such as dills, bread-and-butter, and pickled beets; fermented pickles, such as dill pickles and sauerkraut; refrigerated pickles, such as dills; fruit pickles, such as spiced peaches and crabapples; and relishes, such as corn relish and horseradish.

Bread & Butter Pickles   QE VG GF DF

12 medium cucumbers
8 medium onions, peeled
4 green peppers
¾ C. salt
6½ qts. water
7 C. sugar
6 C. vinegar
3 T. celery seed
¼ C. white mustard seed
1 t. turmeric

Wash cucumbers, onions, and green peppers; slice thin. Soak several hours or overnight in brine made by dissolving the salt in 6 qt. water. Drain. Combine sugar, vinegar, remaining water and spices in large kettle; bring to boil; boil 3 minutes. Add vegetables; boil 20 minutes or until vegetables are clear. Fill into hot sterilized jars. Seal at once. To seal: fill jar, wipe rim with clean, damp cloth, place lid, screw band down tightly.

ⓘInformation: to sterilize/kill bacteria, submerge canning jars, lids, and bands in boiling water for at least 5 minutes.

Refrigerator Dills   Makes about 100 spears

6 - 8 lbs. pickling cucumbers
40 sprigs fresh dill
2 large onions, thinly sliced
5 cl. garlic, sliced
1 qt. water
1 qt. white vinegar
3/4 C. sugar
1/2 C. canning salt

Cut each cucumber lengthwise into four spears. In a large bowl, combine the cucumbers, dill, onions, and garlic; set aside. In a large pot combine the remaining ingredients. Bring to boil, cooking and stirring until salt is dissolved. Pour over cucumber mixture; cool. Cover tightly and refrigerate at least 24 hours. Store in refrigerator up to 2 months.

Leaves & Greens

Basic Ways of Cooking & Serving

Vegetable	Preparation	Cooking Time	Ways to Serve
Lettuce	Refrigerate lettuce and wash as needed to avoid "rusting."		In fresh garden salads.
Mild flavored greens Beet greens, collards, spinach	Save tender young leaves for salads. Remove imperfect leaves and root ends.	Cook in just the water that clings to leaves in saucepan, sauté pan or covered with plastic in microwave. Cook just until wilted and tender.	Buttered with salt, pepper, marjoram, dill weed, mint, rosemary, or minced onion. Or serve with lemon or vinegar, hard-cooked egg slices, crumbled crisp bacon, horseradish, chili sauce, Parmesan cheese.
Strong flavored greens Mustard greens, Swiss chard, turnip greens	Save tender young leaves for salads. Remove imperfect leaves and root ends.	Cook with water to cover. Leave cover off pan to preserve color. Boil tender leaves 5-15 minutes; older thicker leaves 20-25 minutes.	Buttered with salt, pepper, marjoram, dill weed, mint, rosemary, or minced onion. Or serve with lemon or vinegar, hard-cooked egg slices, crumbled crisp bacon, horseradish, chili sauce, Parmesan cheese.

ⓘ **Tip:** leaving the lid off the pan for the first few minutes of cooking helps conserve the green color in vegetables.

Now Add Some Creativity!

Baby Greens with Balsamic Vinaigrette   QE VG GF DF   Serves 6 to 8

1 serving bowl full of mixed baby greens (or torn lettuce leaves)
5 - 6 sliced green onions (use white and green parts)
1T. balsamic vinegar
2 T. olive oil
Salt and pepper to taste

Combine greens and onions. Whisk together the vinegar and oil, then add to salad. Toss to coat leaves. Season to taste.

*ⓘ***Tip:** any flavored vinegar may be used in place of balsamic. Feel free to add other fresh vegetables from the garden, such as tomatoes, sliced carrots, diced cucumber, etc.

Peppery Mustard Greens Salad   QE VG GF DF   Serves 4

4 C. fresh mustard leaves, torn into bite-size pieces
4 green onions, sliced (use green and white parts)
2 T. olive oil
Salt and pepper to taste

Toss all ingredients together and serve.

> *I remember visiting my grandparents in the Yakima Valley in Washington State during my childhood and enjoying all the fresh vegetables they grew in their garden. Nothing was fresher or simpler to make than this salad my grandmother often served.*
>
> *- Jennifer Grant*

Arugula and Beet Salad   QE VG GF DF   Serves 4 or 6

2 - 3 large handfuls of arugula leaves, coarsely chopped
6 fresh beets, roasted, peeled and sliced
4 T. olive oil
2 T. apple cider or wine vinegar
2 T. fresh chives, minced
Salt and pepper to taste

Additional optional ingredients:
½ C. toasted pecans, chopped or ½ C. gorgonzola cheese, crumbled or 1 hard-cooked egg, finely chopped

Combine oil, vinegar, chives, salt, and pepper in a screw-top jar. Cover and shake to blend ingredients. Pour over beets and marinate for 30 minutes. Gently toss with arugula. Add additional optional ingredient of your choice. Gently toss and serve immediately.

ⓘInformation: beets are a good source of folate, manganese, potassium, beta-carotene, and iron.

ⓘTip: avoid large beets that have a hairy taproot. All those tiny hairs on the roots are an indication of age and toughness.

Watercress and Radish Salad   QE VG GF DF   Serves 8

14 C. watercress (about 4 bunches), coarse stems discarded
1½ C. radishes, sliced or julienned
2 T. olive oil
1 T. red-wine or cider vinegar
2 tsp. Dijon mustard
½ tsp. salt
¼ tsp. pepper

This is a great brunch side salad. Try serving it with your favorite quiche recipe.
- Jennifer Grant

Put the olive oil, vinegar, mustard, salt, and pepper in a screw-top jar and shake vigorously to emulsify. Pour dressing into a serving bowl. Add watercress and radishes and toss the salad well.

Tip: try substituting arugula or chopped mustard greens for the watercress.

Fact: gram for gram, watercress contains more vitamin C than oranges, more calcium than milk, more iron than spinach, and more folate than bananas.

Fact: watercress is the most ancient of green vegetables known and can be traced to Greek and Roman times.

Spinach and Pear Salad   QE VG GF   Serves 4

3 C. baby spinach
3 medium ripe yellow pears, cored but not peeled, cut in lengthwise slices
2 T. crumbled blue cheese
2 T. balsamic vinegar
3 T. olive oil
3 T. orange juice
Salt to taste
1 clove garlic, minced
¼ C. chopped walnuts, toasted 5 minutes in 325° oven

Place spinach, pears, and cheese in serving bowl. Whisk together vinegar, olive oil, orange juice, garlic, and salt; pour over and toss with salad. Sprinkle walnuts over the salad while still warm and serve.

Maple Dressed Spinach Salad QE GF DF   Serves 8

10 oz. fresh spinach
4 bacon strips, cooked and crumbled
½ C. tart apple, chopped
½ C. sliced onion
1 C. sliced mushrooms
4 T. maple syrup
3 T. finely chopped green onions
2 T. red wine vinegar
1 T. olive oil
1 T. Dijon mustard
1 clove garlic, minced
Salt and pepper to taste

Place spinach, bacon, apple, onion slices, and mushrooms in a serving bowl. Combine remaining ingredients, except salt and pepper, in a screw-top jar. Shake to blend, then pour over the salad and toss. Season with salt and pepper.

Spinach Rigatoni QE VG   Serves 6

12 oz. uncooked rigatoni pasta (or use penne or ziti)
1½ tsp. olive oil
3 cloves garlic, minced
¾ tsp. salt
¼ - ½ tsp. crushed red pepper (the more you use, the hotter)
1 C. light cream
½ C. crumbled Blue or Gorgonzola cheese
3 C. fresh spinach

Cook pasta according to package directions. Drain pasta, reserving 1 cup cooking liquid. Heat olive oil in a large skillet. Add garlic, salt and crushed pepper; cook 1 minute, stirring so garlic doesn't burn. Stir in cream and blue cheese and cook, stirring constantly for 2 minutes, until slightly thick. Reserved pasta cooking water may be added as needed or to achieve the desired thickness of the sauce. Stir in spinach and pasta; cook about 1 minute, tossing occasionally until spinach wilts and pasta is heated through.

ⓘ **Tip:** vary this rigatoni recipe by adding 3 cups cherry tomato halves when cooking the garlic and seasonings or adding 1/2 cup oven-dried tomatoes (see recipe in Fruiting Vegetables chapter) after spinach wilts. Store-bought sun-dried tomatoes can be used in place of your own oven-dried variety.

Mediterranean Spinach & Rice Salad   VG GF   Serves 6 to 8

1½ C. long grain rice
2½ C. water
1½ tsp. salt
4 T. fresh lemon juice
1/3 C. olive oil
1 clove garlic, minced
1 tsp. fresh oregano or marjoram, minced
¼ tsp. ground pepper
⅛ tsp. red pepper flakes
2 C. chopped spinach
1 red bell pepper, chopped
1 small cucumber, chopped (leave peel on if young and tender)
½ C. chopped green onion
½ C. chopped Italian olives (such as Kalamata)
1 C. crumbled Feta cheese

Put the water in a medium saucepan bring to a boil. Add 1/2 teaspoon salt and the rice. Reduce heat to low, cover the pan, and simmer 15 minutes. Remove rice from the heat and let stand covered for 15 minutes. Uncover and fluff with a fork. In a screw-top jar, put the lemon juice, olive oil, garlic, oregano, pepper flakes, ground pepper, and remaining salt. Shake vigorously to blend. Place the rice in a bowl; pour dressing over and toss to combine. Add the spinach and toss again. Let this mixture sit until no longer steaming, about 20 minutes. Add remaining ingredients and toss to combine. Serve at room temperature or chill and serve cold.

ⓘ **Fact:** spinach is best eaten fresh. It loses nutritional properties with each passing day with half of its major nutrients lost by the week after the day of harvest.

ⓘ **Fact:** spinach is a native plant of Persia (modern day Iran).

Easy Spinach Lasagna Roll-ups VG   Makes 6 Roll-ups

1 large bowlful fresh spinach or Swiss chard, steamed until limp
6 lasagna noodles
8 oz. Ricotta cheese
1 egg, beaten
2 T. Parmesan cheese
½ tsp. seasoned salt
¼ tsp. pepper
⅛ tsp. onion powder
1 C. grated Monterey Jack or Pepper Jack cheese
1 (16 oz.) jar chunky style pasta sauce

Cook noodles according to the package directions; drain. In a small bowl, blend the ricotta cheese, egg, Parmesan cheese, salt, pepper, and onion powder. Stir in spinach and 1 cup jack cheese. Spread the ricotta mixture onto the lasagna strips and roll up. Spread a layer of sauce on the bottom of the baking pan and place the lasagna rolls seam-side-down in the pan. Pour remaining sauce over the top and sprinkle with remaining jack cheese. Cover. Bake in a 350° oven for 45 minutes.

Serve 1 to 2 roll-ups per person.

Tip: vary by adding additional vegetables like sliced mushrooms or zucchini before rolling up.

Creamed Spinach QE VG GF   Serves 4

2 lbs. spinach, stemmed and washed
½ C. heavy cream
½ tsp. salt
Grated nutmeg
Freshly ground pepper

Heat large skillet or Dutch oven over medium heat and cook spinach with a few drops of water until just wilted. Drain and squeeze dry. Chop spinach. In the same skillet, bring cream to a boil. Add salt, nutmeg, and pepper, then stir in chopped spinach. Cook until thickened.

Garlicky Swiss Chard and Beans   QE VG GF   Serves 4

1 T. olive oil
2 cloves garlic, minced
4 C. Swiss chard, rinsed and chopped
¼ C. low-sodium broth
½ tsp. red pepper flakes
1 (15-oz.) can white beans, drained and rinsed
¼ C. grated Parmesan cheese
Balsamic vinegar (optional)

Heat oil in large skillet over medium heat. Add garlic and cook until fragrant, about 30 seconds. Stir in chard, broth, and pepper flakes. Cover and cook over medium heat until chard is wilted and crisp-tender, about 4 minutes. Add beans and heat through. Serve with Parmesan cheese and a splash of balsamic vinegar, if desired. A great side dish to serve with Kielbasa or other type sausage.

*i***Tip:** try substituting kale for the Swiss chard in this recipe.

Baked Sausage, Chard, & Penne Pasta   Serves 4

8 oz. dried penne pasta
1 T. olive oil
8 oz. ground bulk sausage (Italian seasoned, if available)
2 cloves garlic, minced
2 C. Swiss chard leaves
2 C. diced fresh tomatoes (or use a 14-oz. can or diced tomatoes)
¼ tsp. salt
¼ tsp. pepper
8 oz. Mozzarella cheese, shredded
¼ C. grated Parmesan cheese

Preheat oven to 350°. Cook penne pasta in boiling water until tender not soft, about 12 minutes. Drain, reserving some of the pasta cooking liquid. Heat oil in the same pan. Add garlic and sausage, stirring and breaking sausage apart until crumbled and brown, about 10 minutes. Add chard and stir until wilted, about 5 minutes. Stir in tomatoes, salt, pepper and the cooked pasta. Add a little of the pasta water, if mixture seems dry. Pour into a baking dish, sprinkling the top with the Mozzarella and Parmesan cheeses. Bake in oven until heated through, browned and bubbly, about 25 to 30 minutes.

Bacon and Swiss Chard Pasta   QE   Serves 6

16 oz. fettuccini or spaghetti pasta
12 oz. bacon
1 large onion, cut in half lengthwise and sliced
12 C. Swiss chard
1 T. balsamic vinegar
3 T. olive oil
2/3 C. grated Parmesan cheese

Cook pasta in a large pot of boiling salted water until tender but still firm. Drain, reserving 1 cup of the pasta cooking liquid. While pasta is cooking, cook the bacon in a skillet about 10 minutes or until the preferred crispness is reached. Transfer to paper towels to drain. Break into pieces. Drain all but 2 tablespoons of the bacon grease from skillet. Add onion and sauté over medium heat until softened, about 7 minutes. Add Swiss chard and reserved cooking liquid to skillet and toss until chard is wilted and tender, about 4 minutes. Sprinkle with salt, pepper, and vinegar. Cook 1 minute more, then add pasta and olive oil. Toss until coated and heated through. Transfer to a large serving bowl. Sprinkle with bacon and cheese. Season with salt and pepper to taste.

ⓘ **Tip:** try this recipe with spinach in place of the chard.

Indian Greens and Garbanzos   VG GF DF   Serves 4

½ C. low-sodium vegetable broth
1 medium onion, chopped
2 cloves garlic, finely chopped
1 tsp. grated fresh ginger
1 jalapeño pepper, seeded and finely chopped
1 tsp. curry powder
½ tsp. garam masala (Indian spice blend)
1 (15-ounce) can salt-free diced tomatoes
2 (15-ounce) cans salt-free garbanzo beans, drained and rinsed
1 bunch collard greens, stems removed and leaves thinly sliced
½ C. chopped fresh cilantro leaves (optional)
1 T. fresh lemon juice

Heat broth to a simmer in a large skillet over medium-high heat. Add onion, garlic, ginger, and jalapeño and cook until the onion is translucent, about 5 to 6 minutes, stirring occasionally. Stir in the curry and garam masala and cook one more minute. Add tomatoes, garbanzos, and 1 cup water. Bring to a simmer, reduce heat, and simmer 15 minutes. Stir in the collard greens, cover and cook 10 minutes, stirring occasionally until the greens are tender. Stir in the cilantro, lemon juice, and serve.

ⓘ **Tip:** no garam masala in the cupboard? A blend of ½ teaspoon each of cumin, paprika, ¼ teaspoon each cinnamon, cayenne pepper, crumbled bay leaves, and ⅛ teaspoon ground cloves comes close.

ⓘ **Fact:** like kale, cauliflower, and broccoli, collard greens descend from the wild cabbage, a plant thought to have been consumed as food since prehistoric times and to have originated in Asia Minor.

Greens with Roasted Beets Salad   QE VG GF DF   Serves 6 to 8

3 - 4 beets, scrubbed
¼ C. olive oil
1 T. wine vinegar
1 tsp. Dijon mustard
Pinch of sugar
1 small bunch of arugula
1 bunch of watercress
1 small head of butter-type lettuce, torn in bite-size pieces
Sea salt
Pepper

Wash all of the greens, remove tough stems, spin dry. Preheat oven to 450°. Place beets on a baking sheet lined with aluminum foil. Drizzle with one tablespoon oil and season with salt and pepper. Fold aluminum foil up to enclose the beets. Place baking sheet in oven and roast until beets are tender when pierced with the tip of a knife, about an hour. Remove from oven and let stand until no longer too hot to handle. Rub off skins and discard. Cut beets into wedges. Place remaining 3 tablespoons of oil, the vinegar, mustard, sugar, salt, and pepper in a screw-top jar and shake vigorously to blend. Place beets and all of the greens into a bowl. Pour dressing over and toss to combine.

Greens, Beets, and Toasted Walnut Salad   QE VG GF   Serves 8

1/3 C. fresh lemon juice
3 T. sugar
2 T. finely chopped green onions
1 T. olive oil
¼ tsp. salt
1 lb. whole baby beets
½ C. water
8 - 10 C. mixed salad greens
¼ tsp. salt
3 T. chopped walnuts, toasted
3 T. crumbled blue cheese
1 T. fresh chives, chopped

Preheat oven to 375°. Place walnuts on a baking sheet and toast for a few minutes until beginning to brown. Remove from oven and set aside to cool. Combine the dressing ingredients (the first five ingredients listed) in a screw-top jar and shake vigorously to blend; set aside. Place the whole beets in a baking dish; add the water, cover and bake for 35 minutes or until tender. Drain and cool. Rub off skins and cut each beet into quarters. Place in a small bowl and drizzle with 1 tablespoon of the dressing. Arrange salad greens on a platter; sprinkle evenly with salt. Drizzle the remaining dressing over the greens, then top with the beets, walnuts, cheese, and chives. Vary the amounts of dressing ingredients to suit your taste, e.g., less lemon juice, more oil to make less tart.

Mushroom & Barley Soup with Fresh Collards VG DF Serves 10 to 12

2 T. olive oil
2 lbs. fresh mushrooms (any variety), sliced
1 large onion, chopped
1 carrot, peeled and chopped
2 stalks celery, chopped
4 clove garlic, chopped
2 bay leaves
2 T. fresh marjoram (or 2 tsp. dried marjoram or oregano)
1½ tsp. fresh rosemary leaves (or ½ tsp. dried)
2 tsp. salt
½ tsp. pepper
2 C. pearl barley, rinsed
3 quarts vegetable stock (see Bulb, Roots & Tubers chapter for recipe)
1 bunch fresh collard greens

Heat oil in large soup pot over medium-high heat. Add mushrooms, onions, carrot, celery, garlic, bay leaves, marjoram, rosemary, salt, and pepper. Cook until vegetables are significantly soft and stewing in their own juices, about 15 minutes. Stir in barley and stock. Bring soup to a full boil, then reduce to a medium simmer and cook until the barley is tender, about 40 minutes. Meanwhile, cook collard greens separately in boiling water until tender. Remove from water, chop, and set aside. Once barley is tender, add collards to the soup and cook an additional 10 minutes. Season to taste.

ⓘTip: spinach or Swiss chard may be used in place of the collard greens.

Caribbean Bean Soup QE VG GF DF   Serves 4

2 (16.-oz) cans white beans
1 qt. chicken broth (use vegetable stock for vegetarian version)
3 T. cooking oil
1 large onion, chopped
1 green bell pepper, chopped
1 habañero pepper, finely chopped
2 tsp. ground coriander
1 butternut squash, peeled and cut into 1-inch pieces
1 bunch greens (kale, collard, mustard, etc.)
1 C. peanuts (roasted and salted), chopped
Salt to taste
2 T. finely chopped basil

Pour beans (do not drain first) into a soup pot. Add broth and heat to simmering.

In a skillet, stir-fry onion in oil for 5 minutes. Add green pepper and continue stir-frying for another 5 minutes. Lower the heat and add the habañero pepper and coriander and stir-fry for 2 more minutes.

Scrape the pepper mixture to the simmering beans. Add the squash and greens and stir well. Bring mixture to a boil, lower the heat and simmer, covered, for 20 minutes. Add the peanuts to the simmering soup. When the squash is tender, add salt incrementally, to taste. Add fresh basil, stir, and serve.

ⓘ **Tip:** if the soup is too thick, add extra broth, tomato juice, or water.

Fruits, Nuts & Seeds

Creative Ways of Cooking & Serving

ⓘ**Tip:** keep unripe fruit at room temperature to ripen. Store ripe fruit (except pineapple, bananas) in a cool place. Place melons and citrus fruits cut side down on a plate in refrigerator.

ⓘ**Tip:** keep fresh berries wrapped in paper in refrigerator; wash and hull shortly before using.

Now Add Some Creativity!

Apples with Wild Rice and Almonds   VG GF DF   Serves 8

1 large apple, peeled, cored and diced
1 large onion, chopped
½ C. wild rice
½ C. shelled almonds, whole or in slivers
2 T. olive oil
¼ C. raisins or dried cranberries
Salt and pepper to taste
¼ C. parsley or cilantro, chopped

Cook rice in 2½ quarts of salted water until tender, about 40 minutes; drain, saving cooking liquid. Crisp the almonds by toasting them dry (5 to 10 minutes in 350° oven). Heat 1 tablespoon of the olive oil in a large skillet over medium heat. Add onions; cook until soft, about 5 minutes. Add apples, raisins, and a splash of the rice cooking liquid. Cook 5 minutes more until apples are translucent. Combine cooked rice, the apple mixture, nuts, and salt and pepper. Stir in remaining olive oil and serve garnished with cilantro or parsley.

This side dish goes nicely with fish, chicken or pork, and is a good substitute for bread stuffing/dressing. Leftovers can be re-heated, but try eating it cold like a salad.

Old-fashioned Baked Apples VG GF   Serves 4

4 baking apples
8 whole cloves
½ stick butter (2 oz.)
1/3 C. brown sugar
½ tsp. ground cinnamon

Using a small knife, cut a divot from the top of the apples, leaving stem intact. This "cover" will be replaced when baking. Carefully remove seeds and core of the apples. Drop 2 cloves into each apple. Knead together the butter, brown sugar and cinnamon until it is paste-like. Divide paste equally into the cored apples, leaving enough space to replace tops. Place apples in a baking dish with 1/2 cup water on the bottom. Bake at 350° for 1 hour. Sprinkle with cinnamon or powdered sugar before serving.

Country-Style Skillet Apples QE VG GF   Serves 4 to 6

1/3 C. butter
½ C. sugar
½ tsp. cinnamon
2 T. cornstarch, dissolved in 1 C. water
4 cooking apples (Golden Delicious, Rome, Jonagold, Gravenstein)

Peel, core and slice apples; set aside. Melt butter in a skillet over medium heat. Stir in sugar, cinnamon, and cornstarch mixture; mix well. Add apple slices and cook over medium heat, stirring occasionally until tender, about 10 minutes. Serve with pancakes and maple syrup or as a side with grilled breakfast sausages or pork roast at dinner.

Macerated Fruit Salad QE VG GF DF

2 lbs. fruit from the garden (use a variety of apples, pears, berries, cherries, etc.)
4 T. sugar (or to taste)
Juice of ½ to 1 lemon

Cut fruit into pieces or leave whole if small. Layer in a large bowl, sprinkling each layer with sugar and lemon juice, and let the fruit macerate (let stand to soften and become syrupy) for at least an hour.

Homemade Applesauce QE VG GF DF

3 - 4 lbs. apples, peeled, cored, and quartered
1 C. water
Up to 1 C. sugar, depending on desired sweetness (leave out for unsweetened)

Place prepared apples and water in a large pot. Bring to a boil, reduce heat, and simmer until apples are very tender, about 20 to 30 minutes. Remove from heat and mash with a potato masher for chunky sauce or put through a food mill for smooth sauce. Stir in sugar to desired sweetness. Serve hot or chilled. Freezes well; last up to a year in the freezer.

Tip: if using a food mill, skip peeling the apples. The peels will not go through the mill and can simply be discarded.

Tip: apples ripen up to ten times faster at room temperature than if they are refrigerated.

Poached Pears VG GF DF   Serves 6

3 pears, cut in half lengthwise (choose pears that are ripe-firm)
2 C. cranberry or cran-apple juice
2 cinnamon sticks
3 whole cloves
Mint leaves

Remove the peel and seeds from pears. Put all ingredients in a saucepan over medium heat. Be sure the pears are covered with juice. Cook until the pears are soft (easily pierced with a fork), anywhere from 7 to 15 minutes. Remove pears with a slotted spoon and cool on a clean cloth. Lower heat and cook poaching liquid until it is reduced to a third of the original amount. When it is rich and syrupy, remove from the heat. This will take about 45 minutes. To serve, place pears flat side down on plates. Cut and fan the pears out on the plate. Drizzle some of the syrup on top and garnish with mint leaves. Serve warm or chilled.

Tip: for the best quality pears, pick early and allow to ripen indoors. Pick pears when the fruit separates easily from the branch stems.

Cherry Clafoutis QE VG

4 T. unsalted butter
1 lb. fresh sweet cherries, stones removed
1 T. lemon balm leaves, minced
3 eggs
1/3 C. whole wheat flour
1¾ C. low-fat milk

Using a little of the butter, grease a baking dish. Put cherries and lemon balm leaves in the dish. Melt the remaining butter and gently whisk it into the eggs. Whisk the flour into the egg mixture, then the milk. Pour mixture over the cherries and bake until set, about 45 minutes.

Fresh Fruit Tarts QE VG   Serves 6

½ C. sour cream (nonfat or low-fat work fine)
2 T. powdered sugar
1 tsp. chopped fresh mint
1 C. assorted fresh berries or fruit, cut up
1/3 C. lemon yogurt (nonfat or low-fat work fine)
6 small graham cracker crusts (ready-made, single-serve size are available in the supermarket)

In a small bowl, combine sour cream, powdered sugar, and mint. Spoon into graham cracker crusts. Arrange fruit over the sour cream mixture. Cover and refrigerate until serving time. Top with a dollop of lemon yogurt before serving.

Raspberry Sauce VG GF DF   Makes 1½ cups sauce

4 C. fresh raspberries
¼ C. water
¼ C. sugar
½ tsp. fresh lemon juice

Combine first three ingredients in a saucepan over medium-high heat. Bring to a boil, reduce heat and simmer 10 minutes or until slightly thickened.

While simmering, crush the berries with a potato masher. Press the mixture through a sieve into a bowl. Discard the pulp left in the sieve. Add lemon juice to the bowl and stir into the berry sauce. Cover and chill. Will keep five days tightly covered in the refrigerator. Serve as a dessert sauce over your favorite ice cream or pound cake; use in place of syrup over pancakes or French toast; use as an ingredient in salad dressing. This is a very versatile berry sauce.

> *I find the best way to grow raspberries is to use a metal fence post at each "clump" and select 4-5 canes to over winter and cut them off at the top of the fence post - about 5 feet. Tie them to the post with twine. This keeps the canes in a confined space, the canes produce tons of berries and they are easy to pick. They also appreciate a top dressing of chicken manure in the fall.*
>
> *- Kathleen Moore*

Raspberry Bread Pudding QE VG

Serves 4 or 6

8 T. unsalted butter
8 thin slices of bread, crusts removed
3 C. raspberries
2 C. heavy cream
7/8 C. milk
3 large eggs
2 T. brandy (optional)
½ C. superfine sugar

Pre-heat oven to 350°. Butter enough bread to cover the bottom of an ovenproof dish. Place buttered side down in pan and scatter half the raspberries on top. Repeat process with another layer of bread and remaining raspberries. Add one more layer of bread, again place buttered side down.

Mix together cream and milk. Beat in eggs, brandy, and all but 1 tablespoon of the sugar. Pour this mixture over the bread and raspberries. Sprinkle the remaining sugar on top and bake for about 30 minutes, until top is crisp.

(i) **Tip:** pick raspberries only when ripe; they will not further ripen once picked. If you must pull hard to separate the berry from its core, it is not ready for picking!

Frozen Strawberry Jam   QE VG GF DF   Yields 8 half-pints

4½ C. crushed strawberries
2 T. lemon juice
5 C. sugar
1 bottle liquid pectin

To the crushed strawberries add lemon juice and sugar; stir until sugar is dissolved. Add pectin; stir 1 minute. Fill jars, cover with tight fitting lids. Store in the freezer for up to a year. Once opened , keep in the refrigerator for up to a month.

Strawberry Icebox Pie   VG   Serves 6

Crust:
1 C. slivered almonds, toasted (toast in 350° oven until starting to brown)
½ C. graham cracker crumbs
¼ C. sugar
6 T. unsalted butter, melted

Filling:
5 C. hulled and quartered strawberries
1 C. sugar
¼ C. cornstarch
2 T. fresh lemon juice
2 tsp. grated orange peel

1½ C. chilled whipping cream

Preheat oven to 350°. Place almonds in food processor and process until coarsely chopped. Add graham cracker crumbs and sugar; process until finely ground. Add melted butter and process until evenly moistened. Butter a 9-inch glass pie pan. Press crumb mixture onto the bottom and sides of the pie pan. Bake until set, about 12 minutes. Cool completely on a rack.

Place 2 cups strawberries in a medium saucepan. Mash with a potato masher until chunky. Add sugar, cornstarch, and lemon juice. Stir over medium heat until sugar dissolves and mixture boils and thickens, about 3 minutes. Transfer to a mixing bowl and cool to room temperature. Stir in remaining 3 cups of strawberries and the grated orange peel. Mound filling in the crust. Chill pie until cold and set, at least 2 hours and up to 6 hours.

To serve, beat the whipping cream until peaks form. Cut the pie into wedges and serve with a large dollop of the whipped cream.

Strawberry Glacé Pie VG   Serves 6 to 8

6 C. fresh medium-size strawberries
1 C. water
¾ C. sugar
3 T. cornstarch
Red food coloring (optional)
1 baked 9-inch pie shell (recipe follows)

Wash berries; remove hulls. Crush 1 cup of the smaller berries and cook with the water for about 2 minutes. Press through a sieve to remove seeds.

Blend sugar and cornstarch; stir in berry juice. Cook and stir over medium heat until glacé (glaze) is thickened and clear. Stir in about 5 drops of red food coloring, if desired. Spread about ¼ cup glacé on the bottom and sides of the baked pie shell. Arrange half of the whole berries, stem end down, in the pastry shell. Spoon half the remaining glacé carefully over the berries, being sure each is well coated. Arrange remaining berries, stem end down, on first layer; spoon on remaining glacé coating each berry. Chill 3 to 4 hours. To serve, garnish with whipped cream and a few additional berries.

Mom's Pie Crust QE   Makes 2 crusts

2 C. flour
1 t. salt
1/3 C. butter
1/3 C. shortening

Make a paste of 1/4 cup water and 1/3 cup of flour and salt mixture. Cut shortening and butter into flour until it looks like small peas. Mix in the paste until well blended. Divide into 2 disks. Wrap in plastic and refrigerate for 1 hour. This is a never fail dough. Easy!

Strawberry Sauce `QE` `VG` `GF` `DF`   Makes 1¼ cups

2 C. fresh strawberries, hulled
2 T. sugar
2 T. orange juice

Place all ingredients in a blender or food processor and blend until smooth. Serve immediately or cover and refrigerate until serving time. Serve over fresh fruit, pancakes, crepes, waffles, frozen yogurt, or ice cream.

Blueberry Salsa `QE` `VG` `GF` `DF`

2 C. fresh blueberries
½ medium red onion, diced
2 jalapeño peppers, seeded and minced
1 red bell pepper, diced
3 T. cilantro, chopped
¼ C. lime juice
1 tsp. kosher salt

Coarsely chop 1½ cups of blueberries. Combine chopped berries with whole berries and remaining ingredients. Let stand 1 hour.

ⓘ **Information:** hot peppers such as jalapeños contain oils that can burn skin and eyes. Wear plastic gloves when working with them <u>or</u> wash hands really well with soap and water after handling.

ⓘ **Tip:** if you have an abundance of blueberries, pick some to freeze for use during the fall and winter months. Remove any debris, but do not wash the berries! Spread on a baking sheet and place in freezer. Once frozen, transfer berries to a freezer container.

Blueberry & Corn Salad `VG` `GF` `DF`   Serves 6 to 8

6 ears fresh corn, husked
1 C. fresh blueberries
1 small cucumber, sliced
¼ C. finely chopped red onion

¼ C. chopped fresh cilantro
1 jalapeño pepper, seeded and finely chopped
2 T. lime juice
2 T. olive oil
1 T. honey
½ tsp. ground cumin
½ tsp. salt

In a large pot bring water to boiling. Add corn; cook covered for 5 minutes or until tender. When cool enough to handle, cut corn kernels from cob. In serving bowl combine the corn, blueberries, cucumber, onion, cilantro, and jalapeño. Combine remaining ingredients in a screw-top jar. Cover, then shake well to combine. Add to salad and toss. Cover and refrigerate overnight (up to 24 hours).

Mixed Berry Compote   QE VG GF DF   Serves 6

2 C. blueberries
6 T. fresh lemon juice
⅛ tsp. coarse salt
½ C. sugar
1 C. blackberries

Heat blueberries, lemon juice, and salt in a saucepan over medium heat until berries begin to burst, about 4 to 5 minutes. Stir in sugar. Simmer, stirring often until thick enough to coat the back of a spoon, about 6 to 8 minutes. Transfer to a bowl and stir in the blackberries.

Tip: serve this compote with pancakes. It also goes well with chicken, roast pork, or white fish such as halibut.

Fact: blueberries are native to North America where they grow throughout the woods and mountainous regions in the United States and Canada. They were not cultivated until the beginning of the 20th century.

Fact: the blueberry is the second most popular berry in the United States. The strawberry is number one.

Blueberry Tart VG

Serves 10 to 12

Crust:
1¼ C. flour
3 T. (packed) powdered sugar
¼ tsp. salt
10 T. chilled unsalted butter, cut into ½-inch cubes

Filling:
¾ C. sugar
3 T. cornstarch
Pinch of salt
2 T. cold water
2 T. fresh lemon juice
1 T. unsalted butter
1 tsp. grated lemon peel
6 C. fresh blueberries

> *This recipe is one I look forward to making for guests each summer when the blueberries are abundant. I always get rave reviews. Such a decadent dessert, yet so easy to make.*
> *- Jennifer Grant*

Preheat oven to 350°. Place the crust ingredients in a food processor and blend, using on/off turns, until clumps form (this takes awhile). Gather dough into a ball, then press over the bottom and up the sides of a 10-inch tart pan with removable bottom. Pierce all over with a fork. Bake until golden, about 25 minutes. Cool completely.

For filling, whisk the sugar, cornstarch, and salt together in a medium saucepan. Gradually add the cold water and lemon juice, whisking until smooth. Add the butter, lemon peel, and 2 cups berries. Mash coarsely with potato masher. Cook over medium heat until the mixture thickens and boils, stirring occasionally. Remove from heat and fold in remaining berries. Transfer filling into the prepared crust. Refrigerate until cold, at least one hour. Remove tart from pan. Cut into wedges and serve with lightly sweetened whipped cream. Note: tart can be prepared a day ahead. Cover loosely with foil and keep refrigerated.

ⓘ **Information:** blueberries are a good source of vitamin C, potassium, and fiber. They are also a top source of antioxidants.

ⓘ **Fact:** Native Americans called blueberries "star berries," for the blossom's star shape.

Berry Parfaits QE VG GF   Serves 4

2 C. fresh berries (strawberries, raspberries, blueberries, blackberries or a mixture)
2 T. sugar
1 pt. frozen sherbet or yogurt, flavor of your choice

In a bowl, combine berries and sugar. Mash slightly with a potato mashed or fork. Layer berries with sherbet in 4 decorative glasses. Serve immediately or freeze until serving time. If frozen, let stand at room temperature for 10 minutes before serving.

Very Berry Lemonade QE VG GF DF   Makes 13 cups

8 C. cold water
2 C. sugar
3 C. fresh lemon juice (about 15 lemons)
Lemon peel
2 C. fresh berries (strawberries, raspberries, blueberries, blackberries or a mixture)
Lemon slices and/or berries for garnish

Place half the water, the sugar, and generous pieces of lemon peel in a large saucepan. Heat to boiling over high heat, stirring occasionally. Cover saucepan and boil 3 minutes. Remove saucepan from heat.

Purée the berries in a food processor. Pour into a medium-mesh sieve set over a large bowl. Press the berry mixture with the back of a spoon to remove seeds; discard seeds.

Remove the lemon peel from syrup, then stir the syrup into the berry purée. Add the lemon juice and remaining water. Pour into a large pitcher, cover, and refrigerate until cold, at least 3 hours. Serve over ice. Garnish with berries and lemon slices.

ⓘ **Tip:** for a sparkling lemonade, top each glass off with seltzer water or club soda just before serving.

ⓘ **Tip:** a ripe blackberry is a deep black with a plump, full feel. It will pull free from the plant with only a slight tug. If the berry is red or purple, it's not ripe yet.

Berry Herbal Tea `QE` `VG` `GF` `DF`   Makes 6 servings

3 C. water
4 Red Zinger tea bags
1 orange, sliced
1 C. apple or cranberry juice
½ C. fresh strawberries, cut in half or sliced

Put water in a medium saucepan and bring to a boil. Add tea bags and half the orange slices, followed by the juice. Remove from heat; cover and let steep for 3 minutes. Remove tea bags. To serve, place an orange slice in a heat-resistant glass or teacup, along with some of the strawberries. Pour tea (hot or chilled) over the fruit.

Easy Mixed Berry Smoothie `QE` `VG` `GF`   Serves 2

2/3 C. milk (non-fat or low-fat)
1 C. yogurt (low-fat Greek is best)
2 C. strawberries
1 C. raspberries
2 T. honey

Place all ingredients in a blender and blend until puréed and smooth. Stir a few times during the process. Serve immediately.

ⓘ **Tip:** give your smoothie extra zing by adding 1½ teaspoons finely grated ginger with the other ingredients.

Minted Blackberry Ice Tea   QE VG GF DF   Makes about 2 quarts

5 black tea bags
4 C. boiling water
1/2 C. sugar
¼ C. mint leaves, crushed
1 - 1½ C. blackberries, puréed and strained to remove pulp and seeds

Place tea bags, mint, and boiling water in a heat-proof pitcher. Steep for at least 10 minutes. Strain into another pitcher, discarding the mint and teabags. Stir sugar and blackberry purée into the tea. Add more sugar, if sweeter tea is desired. Chill. Serve over ice, garnished with a mint sprig and 2 or 3 blackberries.

Fact: during the Civil War, blackberry tea was said to be a cure for dysentery. During outbreaks, soldiers would "go blackberrying" for blackberries to ward off the disease.

Spiced Pumpkin Seeds   QE VG GF DF

Seeds from one roasted pumpkin (use pumpkin pulp for other recipes)
2 T. olive oil or melted butter
½ tsp. cayenne pepper
2 tsp. paprika
Salt to taste

Place seeds in water and work with your hands to remove the strings. Blot the cleaned seeds with paper towels to remove as much water as possible. Place seeds in a bowl, then add oil and spices and stir to coat. Spread seeds on a cookie sheet and roast in a 350° oven until they are golden and crisp, about 30 to 45 minutes. Stir a couple of times during roasting. Check often towards the end of roasting to make sure the seeds don't burn. Remove from the oven and enjoy this healthy snack.

Tip: try varying the herbs in this recipe, e.g., try garlic powder, seasoned salt, lemon pepper, Cajun seasoning, chili powder, Italian seasoning, or forget the herbs and enjoy the seeds plain (oil and salt only).

Tip: in Latin America, hulled and roasted pumpkin seeds are called pepitas.

Brined Sunflower Seeds VG GF DF

Sunflower seeds are ready to harvest when the yellow petals of the flower have faded and dropped off, and the seeds have started to dry and loosen in the head. If the head gets wet, it will probably mold.

Cut the head with a foot or so of the stem, then hang to dry in a warm place for several days. Remove the seeds from the head and spread on trays to dry awhile longer.

Put the sunflower seeds in brine made of 1½ cups salt and 2 quarts water. If the seeds float, hold then down under the brine with a plate. Soak for 3 days. Drain.

Spread seeds on a baking sheet. Place in 300° preheated oven for 15 minutes, then reduce heat to 250° and toast until dry. Stir every 10 minutes.

Herbs & Edible Flowers

Growing just a few of the classics can give you endless culinary options. Bunch herbs together for a bouquet garni you can use in soups, stews, and sauces. Or grind them into a paste using a food processor or mortar and pestle. Experiment! Add snips of fresh herbs to foods you already make, or add them to bland foods like cream cheese or cottage cheese. Before you know it, you'll wonder how you ever cooked without these garden delights.

Basic Ways of Using

Herb/Flower	Harvesting & Storing	Ways to Serve or Use
Basil	Harvest leaves every week, pinching terminal buds first to encourage branching. Best preserved chopped and frozen or as pesto. Basil keeps well in a glass jar covered with olive oil.	Leaves can be used fresh or dried. Use in egg, fish, pizza, poultry, rice, and vegetable sides recipes. Dried leaves lose their color and flavor, but can be used as tea to aid digestion. Use 1 tsp. of leaf per cup of water.
Bay	Best used fresh, but the leathery leaves can be dried and stored in airtight jars.	Add whole leaves to soups and stews, beans, sauces, stocks, stuffings, fish and poultry. Can be infused as a digestive aid and blended with essential oil for massage into rheumatic joints.
Bee Balm/Bergamot	Harvest leaves for tea just before blooming; dry quickly for best flavor.	Pull petals from flowers and toss fresh in green salad.
Borage	Harvest foliage anytime.	Use raw, steamed or sautéed. Snip blossoms and toss fresh in green salad. Also in chicken, cold soups, fish, and ice tea.
Calendula	Dry petals in shade on paper; store in moisture-proof jars. Whole flowers can be preserved in salad vinegar.	Pull petals from fresh flowers and toss fresh in green salad. Use dried, ground calendula flowers as an inexpensive substitute for saffron in recipes.
Caraway	After blooming, cut plants when seeds are brown, hang upside down in paper bags to dry. Collect seeds and dry a few more days in the sun. Store in tightly sealed container.	Snip tender leaves in spring and use fresh in salads, soups, and stews. Use seeds in bread, cabbage, sauerkraut cauliflower, coleslaw, meatloaf, fish, noodles, pork, potato salad, cooked potatoes, squash, and other recipes.
Chamomile	Collect flowers at full bloom and dry on screens or paper. Store in tightly sealed containers.	Use dried flowers to make a soothing tea.
Chervil	Snip leaves continuously after six to eight weeks; best used fresh.	Good in soups and salads. Leaves are often used with parsley, thyme, and tarragon in French cooking. Add to cooked recipes at the end to preserve flavor.

Chives	Best used fresh or chopped and dried. Freezes poorly.	Use fresh leaf tips all summer in asparagus, carrot, cauliflower, corn, dips, eggs, fish, peas, potatoes, poultry, salad, and soup recipes. Toss pink-lavender flowers in green salad.
Cilantro (leaves) Coriander (seeds)	Harvest foliage before seeds form. Best used fresh - dries and freezes poorly. Gather seeds as they ripen in midsummer.	Use leaves with avocados, bean salads, curries, eggs, fish, potatoes, sauces, soups, stews, stir-fry, tomatoes, and salsas and other Mexican dishes. Use seeds for curries, eggplant, roast pork, salad dressings, shellfish, soups, and other recipes calling for coriander seeds.
Dill	Clip fresh leaves at the stem as needed. Freeze whole leaves or chop first. Dry foliage on nonmetallic screens. Collect flower heads before the seeds fall; hang upside down in paper bags to dry fully. Store harvested seeds in airtight containers.	Can be chopped finely for sauces and used whole as a garnish. Use with avocados, carrots, cucumbers, dips, eggs, fish, green beans, potatoes, pork, poultry, salad and salad dressings, sauces, soups, squash, and stews. Use flower heads (before they go to seed) in green salad. Use seeds in breads, crackers, salad dressings, sauces, soups, stews.
Lavender	Harvest stems that are almost fully in bloom. Spread loosely on a screen to dry or bunch together and hang up-side-down. Remove buds from stems, place in clean cloth bag. Close bag and roll bag, like you would a rolling pin, on flat surface. Scoop buds out of bag and remove any large debris.	Use in soups, stews, ice creams, teas and lemonade. Use flower petals/seeds in baked items such as bread, cakes, frostings, shortbread cookies, and scones.
Lemon Balm	Collect leaves in late summer and dry quickly to prevent them from turning black.	Use fresh in salads or dry for making tea.
Marjoram	Cut fresh leaves as needed for cooking. Hang small bunches to dry, then store in airtight container.	Fresh leaves can be used as a substitute for oregano in recipes. Good in cabbage, carrot, cauliflower, eggplant, egg, fish, lentils and beans, pasta, potato, squash, stuffings, and tomato dishes.
Mint	Harvest fresh leaves as needed. Just before blooming, cut stalks and hang in bunches to dry; store in airtight containers.	Fresh and dried foliage provides flavoring for both sweet and savory dishes. Use in carrot, dessert, eggplant, fruit drinks, fruit salads, lentils and beans, peas, sauces, Tabbouleh and tea recipes. Mint makes a refreshing addition to ice-cold water in summer.
Nasturtium		Snip young fresh leaves and blossoms all summer as needed for salads. In fall, pickle the unopened buds for homemade capers.
Oregano	Snip fresh sprigs as needed all summer. Hang small bunches to dry, then store in airtight container.	Use fresh or dried as called for in Italian and other recipes. Use in beans, eggplant, eggs, fish, pasta, potatoes, salad dressings, sauces, soups, squash, stews, tomatoes, and tomato sauce.
Parsley	Cut leaf stalks at base for fresh foliage all summer. To dry, hang in bunches in shade. Freeze whole or chopped; keep in zippered plastic bags in freezer.	Use fresh or dried as called for in recipes. Goes with just about everything. Traditional garnish.

Herb	Harvest	Uses
Rosemary	Snip fresh foliage as needed all year.	Use sprigs as dry marinade for meats and poultry. Mince to use fresh in recipes. Good with breads, eggs, fish, marinades, pork, potatoes, poultry, soups, squash, stews, and stuffings. An infusion of the leaves can be sipped warm to improve digestion.
Sage	Snip fresh leaves as needed. Bunch them and hang to dry for use during winter months.	Use fresh or dried as called for in recipes. Use with asparagus, beans, cabbage, carrots, corn, eggplant, eggs, fish, ham, peas, pork, potatoes, poultry, sauces, soups, squash, stews, stuffings, and tomatoes.
Savory	Harvest fresh as needed or cut and dry foliage just before flowering.	Use as flavoring in a variety of dishes, teas, herb butters, and vinegars. Use with asparagus, Brussels sprouts, cabbage, carrots, cauliflower, dried beans, eggplant, eggs, fish, peas, poultry, salad dressings, squash, tomatoes.
Tarragon (French)	Snip foliage as needed all summer, or indoors in winter. Fresh foliage lasts several weeks in the refrigerator when wrapped in paper towels, then placed in a plastic bag. Bunch and hang to dry away from sunlight. May also be frozen in zippered plastic bags.	Use in recipes where a hint of licorice is desired. Good with asparagus, broccoli, carrots, cauliflower, chicken, eggs, fish, peas, potatoes, rice, salad dressings, sauces, tomatoes. Place fresh sprig in bottle when making vinegars.
Thyme	Snip foliage as needed in summer. Bunch together and hang to dry or strip the leaves and dry on a screen. Foliage freezes well in airtight containers or bags.	Enriches the flavor of meats or soups. Also good with asparagus, broccoli, carrots, corn, dried beans, eggplant, eggs, fish, green beans, peas, poultry, rice, stuffings, and tomatoes. Use a sprig as a garnish.
Violet	Thoroughly dry flowers for culinary use. Store in airtight containers.	Petals may be added to fruit salads, flans, and jams or candied and used to decorate cakes and desserts.

Now Add Some Creativity!

Fresh Greens with Thyme Dressing   Makes 2 cups dressing

1 T. fresh thyme leaves
½ C. olive oil
½ C. buttermilk
1 C. mayonnaise
¼ tsp. minced garlic
1 tsp. sea salt

Whisk all the ingredients together by hand. Refrigerate. Use to dress fresh garden greens.

ⓘ **Information:** *infusion* is the extract of an herb made by steeping or soaking the flowers, leaves, and stems of the plant in boiling water.

ⓘ **Tip:** fresh bouquets of such herbs as parsley, sage, basil, oregano, rosemary, and thyme can be stored in a glass of water in the refrigerator. Cover loosely with clear plastic bag to keep herbs fresh as water condenses inside the bag.

Flowery Greens   QE VG GF DF   Serves 4 to 6

1 serving bowl full of mixed baby greens (or torn lettuce leaves)
1 C. edible flowers (calendula petals, bee balm petals, nasturtium flowers, dill
    heads, chive flowers)
1T. rice vinegar
2 T. olive oil
Salt and freshly ground pepper

> *This simple salad is one of our summertime favorites, so refreshing and colorful.*
> *- Jim Grant*

Whisk together the rice vinegar and olive oil and toss with the greens and flowers. Salt and pepper to taste.

Green Rice Pilaf   QE VG GF   Serves 4

3 T. butter
2 C. chopped onion
2 C. long-grain rice
½ C. packed fresh herbs such as chives, tarragon, parsley, dill
4 C. vegetable stock (see Bulb, Roots & Tubers chapter for recipe)
Salt and pepper to taste
1 bay leaf

Melt butter in a medium saucepan over medium heat. Add onion; cook until translucent, about 5 minutes. Add rice; cook, stirring often, until rice is well coated and golden in color.

In a blender, combine the herbs, stock, salt, and pepper. Blend until herbs are finely chopped. Add herbed stock to rice; bring to a boil, add bay leaf, and then lower heat to maintain a very slow simmer. Cover tightly and cook until rice has absorbed all liquid, about 25 minutes. Fluff with a fork, replace cover, and let stand for 5 minutes before serving.

Herby Green Beans QE VG GF DF

Serves 4

1 lb. fresh green beans, ends removed
2 T. extra virgin olive oil
¼ C. chopped fresh parsley
1½ tsp. chopped fresh basil leaves
1½ tsp. chopped fresh oregano leaves
⅛ tsp. crushed red pepper
2 cloves garlic, minced
Salt

Boil beans in salted water for 5 minutes uncovered. Cover and cook 5 to 10 minutes longer until crisply tender. Drain. Heat oil in large skillet. Cook and stir remaining ingredients until garlic is golden. Add beans and cook 1 to 2 minutes, stirring occasionally, until beans are hot and coated with herb mixture.

T J Dilly Bread VG

Makes 1 loaf

2¼ tsp. active dry yeast
¼ C. warm water (105°)
1 C. cottage cheese, heated to lukewarm
3 T. Asiago or Parmesan cheese, grated
2 T. olive oil
2 T. dill seeds
1 tsp. salt
½ tsp. black pepper
1 egg, well-beaten
2½ C. flour, more or less

We never miss having this bread with holiday meals.

- Linda Bondurant

Dissolve the yeast in the warm water. In a large bowl, combine the warmed cottage cheese, egg, oil, dill seeds, salt, and pepper, Asiago or Parmesan. Add the yeast and stir in flour. Cover and let double, about 50 to 60 minutes. Punch down and put in a well-greased 8-inch pan or casserole dish. Let rise about 30 to 45 minutes, then bake in a preheated 350° oven for 35 to 40 minutes. Remove from oven and let cool for 5 minutes. Remove from pan and brush with butter and a sprinkle of coarse salt.

Soft Herb Rolls VG

Makes 12 rolls

1 (¼-oz.) pkg. active dry yeast
3 T. sugar
1 tsp. table salt
1 T. each 4 different herbs (such as minced flat-leaf parsley, fresh dill, chives, basil marjoram, or rosemary)
2 T. melted butter
1 extra large egg, beaten (save out 1 tablespoon and beat well - will be used after rolls are shaped)
1 C. milk
3½ - 3¾ C. flour
1 T. sea salt or coarse kosher salt

Sprinkle yeast over 1/4 cup cool (70°) water. Let stand until dissolved, about 5 minutes. Stir in sugar, table salt, herbs, melted butter, egg, and milk. Add 3¼ cups flour and stir to moisten. Knead dough on a lightly floured surface until elastic and not sticky, adding flour as needed to prevent sticking. Knead for about 15 minutes. Shape into 12 balls and place in a greased 9 x 13-inch pan. Let dough rise in a warm place until doubled, 45 - 60 minutes.

Brush rolls with the reserved beaten egg and sprinkle with coarse salt. Bake in a preheated 350° oven until a deep golden color, about 25 to 30 minutes.

Rosemary Focaccia Bread VG DF

Serves 6 to 8

1 (4-oz.) pkg. active dry yeast
1 1/3 C. warm water
3¾ C. flour
½ C. olive oil
1 T. plus 1 tsp. sea salt
1 tsp. sugar
1 T. rosemary, minced plus 1 T. rosemary, coarsely chopped

Combine the yeast and warm water in a small bowl (be sure bowl is not cold) and stir to dissolve. Set aside for 5 minutes. Combine the flour, 2 tablespoons of the oil, 1 tablespoon of the sea salt, the sugar, and minced rosemary in a large bowl. Add the yeast mixture and stir with a wooden spoon to blend. Knead for 10 minutes by hand.

Brush the inside of a large clean bowl with oil and transfer the dough to the bowl, pressing and turning over to coat all sides of the dough with oil. Cover with plastic wrap, placing it on the dough inside the bowl, so it rises with the dough. Set aside to rise until double, about 1½ hours.

Punch dough down. Turn dough onto a floured work surface; press the dough into a rectangle measuring about 9 x 12 inches, then roll with a rolling pin until dough is 10 x 14 inches. Transfer dough to a greased baking sheet. Stretch to keep dough at 10 x 14 inch measurement. Brush top of dough with oil, cover with plastic wrap, and let rise for 1½ hours.

Preheat oven to 400°. Five minutes before baking the bread, press "dimples" into the surface with your fingertips, about ¾-inch deep and 2 inches apart. Drizzle with remaining oil (about 1/3 cup) and sprinkle with the chopped rosemary and sea salt. Bake on the center rack of the oven for 20 minutes, then lower heat to 350° and bake another 25 minutes, or until the top is crisp and golden brown. Cool on the pan for 10 to 15 minutes, then transfer to a wire rack. Serve warm or at room temperature. Cut into squares before serving.

Tip: use dill seeds that you've dried from the dill plants in your garden for recipes that call for deed seed. To dry, collect the seed heads, place them head first into a paper bag, then secure the bag and hang upside down by the dill stems. As the seeds dry they will drop into the inverted bag. Remove the seeds from the bag and spread on a tray to dry for 10-14 days. Store in airtight container. Do not dry in a plastic bag!

Fact: since Antiquity, rosemary has had a reputation for strengthening memory. Because of this, it became a symbol of fidelity for lovers. Rosemary holds a special place among herbs for symbolism - *Rosemary for Remembrance* - and is used at not only weddings, but at funerals and as incense in religious ceremonies.

Tip: sage quickly becomes a small woody shrub that can need replacing every 3 to 4 years. Frequent harvesting and pruning helps to reinvigorate sage plants.

Herbed Biscuits QE VG Makes about twenty 1¾-inch biscuits

2 C. flour
3 tsp. baking powder
1 tsp. salt
6 T. shortening
2/3 C. milk
2 T. fresh herbs, minced (rosemary, sage, marjoram, parsley, thyme, lavender buds, etc.)

Pre-heat oven to 450°. Measure and mix dry ingredients in a bowl. Cut in shortening with a pastry blender until mixture looks like "meal." Stir in the minced herbs and almost all of the milk. Too much milks makes biscuits sticky, not enough makes biscuits dry. Add remaining milk if dough is too dry. Empty dough onto a floured cloth or board and knead lightly for about 30 seconds. Roll out to about ½-inch thickness and cut with a biscuit cutter. Arrange biscuits on an ungreased baking sheet and place in the middle of the oven; bake for 10-12 minutes. Serve piping hot!

Herbed Cheese Spread QE VG GF Makes about 1¼ cup spread

1 (8-oz.) pkg. cream cheese
2 T. butter, softened
1 T. Worcestershire sauce
1½ tsp. cream
1 tsp. lemon juice
1 small clove garlic, minced
½ - 1 tsp. (based on your likes) of each of the following fresh herbs, minced: chives, parsley, dill weed, basil, thyme, tarragon
¼ tsp. celery seeds
2 dashes hot pepper sauce
Salt and pepper to taste

Mix cream cheese and butter in food processor or by hand. Add remaining ingredients and process or stir by hand until well blended. Add more cream, if needed, to smooth out mixture. Spoon into cheese crock or other container and refrigerate overnight. Serve at room temperature with crackers or toasted baguette slices.

Herby White Bean Spread   QE VG GF DF   Makes about 3 cups spread

2 T. olive oil
1 onion, chopped
3 cloves garlic, minced
1 T. chopped fresh tarragon leaves (or combination of fresh tarragon & rosemary leaves)
2 (15-oz.) cans white beans, drained
2 T. white wine vinegar
⅛ tsp. cayenne
Salt
Freshly ground pepper
Rosemary or tarragon sprigs for garnish

Preheat oven to 350°. Heat oil in a medium skillet over medium heat. Add the onion and sauté until soft, not brown, about 5 minutes. Lower heat and add garlic and tarragon/rosemary; sauté until fragrant, about 2 minutes. Remove from heat and scrape into the bowl of a food processor. Add beans, vinegar, cayenne, salt and pepper, then process until smooth. Taste; adjust seasoning as desired. Transfer mixture to an oiled baking dish. Smooth the top and drizzle with a little olive oil. Bake uncovered until hot, about 25 minutes. Garnish with rosemary or tarragon sprigs. Serve with slices of baguette.

Simple Herb Butter   QE VG GF   Makes 1/4 cup

1 T. minced fresh herbs, washed and dried well
4 oz. butter, softened

Mix ingredients together by hand or electric mixer. Chill for at least three hours before serving. Store wrapped tightly in plastic for up to one month in the refrigerator, or keep frozen for up to three months.

ⓘ**Tip:** use herbs singly or in combinations. Try mint with dill, dill with garlic, chives with marjoram. Dried herbs may be substituted; use 1½ teaspoons dry per tablespoon of fresh herbs.

ⓘ**Tip:** hardy herbs like rosemary, marjoram, and sage will stay fragrant for a week.

Lemony Nasturtium Butter QE VG GF

Makes 3/4 cup

½ C. unsalted butter (room temperature)
2 tsp. grated lemon peel
1 T. lemon juice
3 T. finely chopped nasturtium flowers

Mix all ingredients until smooth and well blended. Refrigerate or freeze until ready to use. Great with broccoli or asparagus, also with chicken or fish.

Fact: cooks in Italy and southern France consider the nasturtium a green vegetable.

Fresh Herb Mayonnaise QE VG GF

Makes about ½ cup

½ C. mayonnaise
1 tsp. minced fresh chives
1 tsp. minced fresh dill
1 tsp. minced fresh tarragon
1 tsp. minced fresh scallion (green onion), white part only

Whisk the herbs into the mayonnaise. Excellent with cold roasted chicken, tuna, or hard-cooked eggs. Use in place of plain mayonnaise on your favorite sandwich.

Pesto Sauce QE VG GF

Serves 8

1 large bunch fresh basil, stems removed
5 cloves garlic
½ C. pine nuts, toasted to a very light brown
2 C. olive oil
½ C. grated Parmesan cheese
Coarse salt and freshly ground pepper

Pulse garlic in food processor until finely chopped. Add nuts and pulse to break into pieces. Scrape sides of bowl. Pile in all the basil. Pour half the olive oil over the leaves and pulse until basil is chopped. Transfer to a mixing bowl and fold in Parmesan cheese. Season with salt and pepper and adjust sauce consistency with remaining olive oil. Keep in refrigerator up to a week or in the freezer for up to 2 months.

ⓘ **Tip:** experiment with this pesto recipe by using different nuts or replacing all or part of the basil with other fresh herbs such as parsley.

Herbed French Dressing QE VG GF DF

2 T. minced fresh herbs, washed and dried well
¾ C. olive oil
¼ C. vinegar

Shake all ingredients together.

Herb & Yogurt Dressing QE VG GF

2 T. minced fresh herbs, washed and dried well
1 C. plain yogurt

Shake all ingredients together.

Herbal Honey QE VG GF DF

1 T. fresh herbs, washed and dried well <u>or</u> 1½ tsp. dried herbs <u>or</u> ½ tsp. herb seeds
2 C. honey

Bruise herbs slightly and place in a muslin bag or directly into a saucepan. Pour the honey into pan and heat until just warm (high heat will spoil it). Pour into hot, sterilized jars and seal. Store at room temperature for a week, then re-warm honey and strain out the herbs. Return honey to hot, sterilized jars and seal. You can leave the herbs in for texture and color.

Nasturtium Vinegar QE VG GF DF   Makes 1 pint vinegar

1 pt. white wine, apple cider or champagne vinegar
1 C. nasturtium leaves, flowers and buds

Place ingredients in a clear glass bottle or jar, tightly seal, and let stand for 3 weeks before using. Flowers may remain in the vinegar, but be sure they are covered with vinegar to avoid molding. Great for use in salad dressings and sauces; nice peppery flavor.

Herbed Salt QE VG GF DF

1 C. sea salt or kosher salt
1 C. packed fresh herbs, washed, dried, and minced (or 2 T. dried)

Grind the salt and herbs together in a blender, or finely crumble the herbs by hand, then mix with salt. Store in an airtight jar or place mixture in a shaker and use to add flavor to your meals.

Tip: herbed salt can add instant flavor to your oils and dressings and help you reduce actual salt use.

Herbal Tea QE VG GF DF

2½ oz. fresh herbs or 1 oz. dry
2 C. water

Chop fresh herbs finely so their flavor and medicinal properties will be released. Place herbs in a teapot and pour boiling water over them. Cover tightly and let steep for at least 10 minutes. Strain into teacups.

Tip: try flavoring your herbal teas with honey, lemon juice and zest, orange juice and zest, cinnamon sticks.

Lavender Shortbread QE VG   Makes about 2 dozen cookies

¾ C. butter, softened
¼ C. sugar
2 C. flour
¼ C. lavender flowers & buds

Thoroughly mix butter and sugar. Add flour and lavender and work in with hands. Chill. Roll dough until ¼ to ½ inch thick. Cut with a small biscuit cutter or cookie cutters. Place on an ungreased baking sheet and bake in a 350° oven for 20 to 25 minutes.

Tip: the tops of shortbread cookies will not brown, and the shape of the cookies will not change. Do not leave these cookies in the oven too long, thinking there will be some change in color or shape.

Gifts from the Garden

Now Add Some Creativity!

Rosemary Oil   QE VG GF DF

1 C. oil
1 T. fresh rosemary leaves

Put leaves in a mortar or a bowl with a little of the oil. Pound or muddle gently to release flavors. Add this to the rest of the oil and pour into a tight-fitting screw-top jar. Leave on a sunny window sill for 3 weeks, shaking gently every day or so. Strain through muslin and pour into any bottle that has a screw top or stopper/cork. Finish by adding a fresh sprig of rosemary to the bottle. Use oil with poultry and in pasta dishes.

ⓘTip: Rosemary oil is delicious rubbed on meat before grilling.

Herbal Oil   QE VG GF DF

¼ C. packed fresh herbs, washed and dried well
1 C. olive or vegetable oil

Bruise herbs slightly to release flavors, then place in the bottom of a hot, sterilized jar. Heat the oil in a saucepan until just warm, then pour into the jar. Let the flavored oil cool, then cover tightly and store in the refrigerator.

ⓘTip: Basil oil is excellent with fresh or cooked tomatoes and on pasta. Dill oil gives flavor to hot, boiled potatoes.

Basic Herbal Vinegar QE VG GF DF

1 - 2 C. packed fresh herbs, washed and dried well or 2-3 T. herb seeds
4 C. vinegar (5% acidity)

Wash and dry the herbs (any leftover water will turn the vinegar cloudy), then pack into hot, sterilized glass jars using a wooden spoon. Fill with vinegar, leaving 1 inch at the top. With the spoon, push the herbs down and lightly bruise them. If using seeds, first gently bruise them using a mortar and pestle before putting in jars. Cover tops of the jars with tightly placed plastic cling wrap before putting on metal lids (to prevent chemical reactions between vinegar and metal). Screw metal lid tight. Let herbs steep in a warm, dark place, such as a cupboard near the stove or on a shelf near fireplace, for three to six weeks. Strain the flavored vinegar through a paper coffee filter. Bring vinegar to a boil, then pour into hot, sterilized jars or decorative bottles. Add a few fresh sprigs of same herbs and cap. Seal bottle by turning over and dipping top into melted paraffin. Dip a few times to build up the wax seal.

Try these combinations:

Tarragon in red wine vinegar
Basil, oregano and thyme in red wine vinegar
Rosemary in white wine vinegar
Chive flowers in white wine vinegar
Thyme and garlic in sherry vinegar

Tip: avoid using distilled white vinegar because it has no flavor.

Herb Bath Sachets

Combine dried lavender, rose petals, sage, and rosemary in a muslin bag. Tie the bag under the faucet of your bathtub and let the water run through it, or float it in the water to scent your bath. When you find a favorite combination of herbs, make several to give as gifts. Keep a basket or bowl full of bath sachets handy by the tub.

Herbal Soap

1 block of glycerin soap base (available at most craft stores), grated
3 T. chopped flower petals or fresh herbs
Distilled water

Evenly distribute the grated glycerin in a pot (designated for soap making only). Pour in enough distilled water to cover the glycerin. Place pot on the stove and heat until the glycerin is completely melted. Stir throughout this process. Once completely melted, remove the pot from the stove and add the flowers/herbs. Stir to distribute the flowers evenly throughout the soap. Pour mixture into soap molds. Once it hardens, it is ready to use.

Potpourri

Traditional potpourri is a mixture of dried flower petals and other ingredients, placed in open containers and positioned to allow the mixture's aroma to delicately scent the room. Gather flowers from the garden; those especially good to use in potpourri are roses, carnations, violets, sunflowers, statice, calendula, marigold, peony, honeysuckle, nasturtium, lily of the valley, white jasmine, and lavender. Some herbs such as mint, chamomile, thyme, sage, and rosemary also work well. Don't limit yourself ~ use your imagination and experiment with whatever you have growing in the garden.

Pick flowers, allow to dry for awhile. Separate the petals and continue drying until all moisture is gone and petals feel dry. Be careful not to dry in direct sun, as this will cause the flower's colors to fade. Remove petals and mix the various petals. Potpourri ingredients should not be finely ground, but lightly crushed. Leave some petals whole for decorative touch.

Rose Water

3 C. rose petals
3 C. purified water

Pick rose petals in the morning after the dew has dried. Place in a glass container and pour boiling water over the petals. Allow to steep for two days, stirring frequently. Strain and bottle. Rosewater gives food and drinks a distinct, rosy flavoring and smell.

Herbal Sachets

To create herbal sachets, tie beautiful ribbons on muslin bags filled with lavender, rose petals, chamomile, and calendula. Place in dresser drawers, hang in closets, slip under your pillow.

Aromatic Kitchen Hot Pads

Pulverize your favorite kitchen herbs and spices. Fill pads sewn out of heavy fabric with the herb mixture. The heat from a hot dish sitting on the pad will release the kitchen sachet's aroma.

Moth-proof Sachets

Fill a sachet bag with cedar chips, lavender, mint, and rosemary to moth-proof dresser drawers and closet.

Sunflower Backyard Bird Treat

When sunflower seeds are ready to harvest (yellow petals of the flower have faded and the seeds have started to dry out), cut the head with a foot or so of stem and hang to dry in a warm place for several days. Once dry, cut off the stalk, and drill a hole through the face of the sunflower near the top. Thread a nice ribbon through the sunflower head and tie a bow, leaving space between the sunflower and bow for hanging. Hang in a tree during the winter for the birds to enjoy or give as a gift to someone who cares about our fine-feathered friends.

Wild Bird Garland Treats

To make these garlands, use apples, pears, grapes, berries, summer squash or any other fresh fruits you have around the garden. Slice large items into manageable sizes. Poke a hole in the center of each piece of fruit. Tie a large knot in one end of a 3 to 4 foot piece of twine. Run the twine through the pieces of fruit and vegetables. Hang the garland over a tree branch for your feathered friends to feast on.

Cranberry & Popcorn Bird Treats

Poke holes in dried cranberries and popped corn, then string on a piece of thin twine. Hang from the trees for your backyard wild bird visitors. A welcome winter treat!

The Cook's Helpers

Culinary Terms

Al dente - cooked so as to be firm, but not hard as in pasta; crisp-tender as in vegetables.

Au beurre - to cook with or in butter.

Au gratin - to cook with a browned covering of bread crumbs, often mixed with butter or cheese.

Bake - to cook by dry heat in oven.

Baste - to moisten food while cooking, usually by dipping pan juices over meat that is being roasted, uncovered, in the oven.

Beat - to mix with vigorous over-and-over motion with spoon, whip, or beater.

Blanch - to cook partially, or precook by plunging into rapidly boiling water for just a few minutes. Then remove, drain, and cool.

Blend - to mix thoroughly.

Boil - to cook in steaming liquid in which bubbles are breaking on the surface.

Bouquet garni - a bunch of herbs (commonly bay leaf, thyme, parsley) tied together with a string or in a muslin bag; used in cooking of soups, stews, and sauces; removed before serving.

Braise - to cook slowly in a covered pan in a small amount of liquid.

Bread - to coat food with bread crumbs or a combination of bread crumbs, milk, and egg.

Broil - to cook by direct heat, under or over a gas flame, electric broiler, or glowing charcoal.

Caramelize - to cook until a deeply browned color is reached.

Chiffonade - to produce fine ribbons by stacking vegetable or herb leaves, then rolling tightly and cutting across with a sharp knife.

Chop - to cut in fine or coarse pieces using a sharp knife or food chopper.

Coddle - to cook briefly until "set" but not hard in boiling water.

Cream - to rub or work shortening or butter and sugar against side of bowl with spoon or by beating with mixer until thoroughly blended and creamy.

Cut in - to incorporate fat into flour mixture using a pastry blender, fork, or two knives.

Deep-fry - to cook foods by immersing in boiling fat or oil, usually at 365°.

Dredge - to coat thickly with flour or flour mixture.

De-glaze - to add a liquid (broth, marinade, or wine) to a pan to loosen and dissolve the brown bits and pan drippings at the bottom of a pan that form during cooking. This pulls all the flavor possible out of the cooking process.

Fines herbes - a mixture of minced fresh herbs, such as basil, chives, marjoram, tarragon, and thyme, stirred into foods at the end of cooking to add color and flavor.

Fold in - to cut down through center of batter with edge of spoon, rubber scraper, or spatula, bringing up close to side of bowl, then lightly turning over, cutting down through again. Turn bowl a quarter turn at same time. Repeat until ingredients are blended.

Grate - to rub against a grater to shred food.

Grind - to cut or crush in a food grinder/processor.

Infusion - the extract of an herb made by steeping or soaking the flowers, leaves and stems of the plant in boiling water.

Julienne - to cut into thin strips.

Knead - to press dough with heel of hand, alternately folding and pushing and stretching it.

Macerate - to soak a food in liquid to soften or dissolve it; let stand to become soft and syrupy.

Marinade - to let food stand in oil-acid mixture for added flavor or to tenderize.

Mince - to chop or cut into very small pieces.

Mix - to combine ingredients, as by stirring.

Pan-broil - to cook on an ungreased hot surface.

Pan-fry - to cook in a small amount of fat or oil.

Parboil - to partially cook food in boiling water; the cooking is then completed by another method.

Poach - to cook in simmering water.

Purée - to liquefy food by forcing through a fine strainer or by use of a food mill or blender/processor.

Render - to free fat from connective tissue over low heat.

Roast - to cook by dry heat, usually in the oven.

Roux - a cooked mixture of flour and butter used to thicken sauces or main dishes.

Sauté - to fry lightly in a small amount of fat, stirring constantly.

Scald - to heat to just below the boiling point until a skin forms over the top, as with milk.

Score - to cut narrow gashes part way through outer surface of food.

Sear - to brown surface quickly.

Shred - to tear or cut into small, but long narrow pieces.

Sift - to pass through a sieve to remove lumps or blend dry ingredients together.

Simmer - to cook in water just below the boiling point.

Sliver - to cut or shred into long thin pieces.

Steam - to cook over but not in boiling water. Usually food is placed in a wire basket or perforated metal device which is placed in a covered saucepan containing a small amount of boiling water.

Steep - to allow food to stand in broth, seasoned liquid or water that is hot, but not boiling.

Stew - to cook slowly in liquid.

Veganism - a type of vegetarian diet that excludes meat, eggs, dairy products and all other animal-derived ingredients.

Vegetarianism - the practice of following plant-based diets (fruits, vegetables) with or without the inclusion of dairy products or eggs, and with the exclusion of meat, poultry, and seafood. Abstention from by-products of animal slaughter, such as animal-derived rennet and gelatin may also be practiced.

Whip - to beat rapidly to produce expansion through the incorporation of air, as in egg whites and whipping cream.

Recipe Abbreviations

c. = cup
pt. = pint
qt. = quart
gal. = gallon
tsp. = teaspoon
T. = tablespoon
lb. = pound
oz. = ounce
sl. = slice
bu. = bunch
cl. = cloves

med. = medium
lg. = large
fl. = fluid
pkg. = package
pkt. = packet
env. = envelope
doz. = dozen
hr. = hour
min. = minutes
sq. = square

Weights & Measures

3 teaspoons = 1 tablespoon or 1/2 ounce
1/2 tablespoon = 1½ teaspoons
2 tablespoons = 1/8 cup or 1 ounce
4 tablespoons = 1/4 cup or 2 ounces
5 tablespoons plus 1 teaspoon = 1/3 cup
8 tablespoons = 1/2 cup or 4 ounces
10 tablespoons plus 2 teaspoons = 2/3 cup
12 tablespoons = 3/4 cup or 6 ounces
16 tablespoons = 1 cup or 8 ounces
2 cups = 1 pint
4 cups = 1 quart
2 pints = 1 quart
4 quarts = 1 gallon
1 ounce = 1/8 cup or 2 tablespoons
8 ounces = 1 cup or 16 tablespoons
16 ounces = 1 pint   16 ounces = 1 pound

Metric Equivalents

U.S. to Metric

Capacity

1/5 teaspoon = 1 milliliter
1 teaspoon = 5 ml
1 tablespoon = 15 ml
1/5 cup = 50 ml
1 cup = 240 ml
2 cups (1 pint) = 470 ml
4 cups (1 quart) = .95 liter
4 quarts (1 gal.) = 3.8 liters

Weight

1 fluid oz. = 30 milliliters
1 fluid oz. = 28 grams
1 pound = 454 grams

Metric to U.S.

Capacity

1 milliliters = 1/5 teaspoon
5 ml = 1 teaspoon
15 ml = 1 tablespoon
34 ml = 1 fluid oz.
100 ml = 3.4 fluid oz.
240 ml = 1 cup
1 liter = 34 fluid oz.
1 liter = 4.2 cups
1 liter = 2.1 pints
1 liter = 1.06 quarts
1 liter = .26 gallon

Weight

1 gram = .035 ounce
100 grams = 3.5 ounces
500 grams = 1.10 pounds
1 kilogram = 2.205 pounds

Fahrenheit or Celsius?

To convert a Fahrenheit temperature to Celsius:

1. subtract 32
2. multiply by 5
3. divide by 9

To convert a Celsius temperature to Fahrenheit:

1. multiply by 9
2. divide by 5
3. add 32

Common Food Equivalents

Flour (all-purpose):	4 cups sifted = 1 pound
Flour (cake)	4½ cups sifted = 1 pound
Flour (whole wheat)	3½ cups = 1 pound
Flour (rye):	4½ to 5 cups = 1 pound
Corn meal:	1 pound = 3 cups
Confectioner sugar:	3 to 4 cups sifted = 1 pound
Granulated sugar:	2¼ to 2 1/3 cups = 1 pound
Brown sugar:	2¼ cups firmly packed = 1 pound
Butter:	1 pound = 2 cups
	1 stick = 1/2 cup, 1/4 pound or 8 tablespoons
	1 ounce = 2 tablespoons
Cheese:	1 pound = 4 to 5 cups shredded
	1/4 pound (4 ounces) = 1 cup shredded
	1 pound = 2 2/3 cups cubed
Blue cheese:	4 ounces crumbled = 1 cup
Cream cheese:	3-oz. pkg. = 6 tablespoons
Whipping cream:	1 cups = 2 cups whipped
Evaporated milk:	6 ounce can = 2/3 cup
	14 ounce can = 1 2/3 cup
Eggs:	4 to 6 whole, shelled = 1 cup
Egg whites:	8 to 10 whites = 1 cup
Egg yolks:	12 to 14 yolks = 1 cup
Apples:	1 pound = 3 medium
	1 medium = 3/4 to 1 cup chopped
	2 medium = about 1½ cups
	1 large = 1 cup chopped
Lemons:	1 medium = 2 to 3 tablespoons juice
	5 to 8 medium = 1 cup juice
Lemon rind (grated):	1 medium lemon = 1½ teaspoons finely grated
	1 medium lemon = 1 tablespoons coarsely grated
Oranges:	1 medium = 2 to 3 tablespoons juice
	3 to 4 medium = 1 cup juice
Orange rind (grated):	1/2 orange = 1 teaspoon finely grated
	1/2 orange = 1 tablespoon coarsely grated
Banana:	1 pound = 3 medium
	3 medium = 1 to 1 1/3 cups mashed

Berries:	1 pint = 1 3/4 cups
Raisins:	1 pound = 3 cups, loosely packed
Onions:	1 medium = 1/2 cup chopped
	8 green sliced = 1 cup
Tomatoes:	1 pound = 3 medium
	100 grape tomatoes = about 4 cups
Dried white beans:	1 pound = 2 cups uncooked = 6 cups cooked
Dried kidney beans:	1 pound = 2 2/3 cups uncooked = 6¼ cups cooked
Dried lima beans:	1 pound = 3 cups uncooked = 7 cups cooked
Long grain rice:	1 pound = 2 cups uncooked = 6 cups cooked
Macaroni:	8 ounces = 2 cups uncooked = 4 cups cooked
Egg noodles:	8 ounces = 2½ uncooked = 4 to 5 cups cooked
Spaghetti:	8 ounces = 2½ uncooked = 4 to 5 cups cooked
Popcorn:	1/4 cup kernels = 8 cups popped
Bread crumbs:	1 pound fresh bread crumbled = 9 cups crumbs
	1 pound dry bread crumbled = 3½ cups crumbs
	2 slices bread = 1 cup soft crumbs
Cracker crumbs	38 saltines crushed = 1 cup crumbs
	14-15 graham crackers = 1 cup crumbs
	22 vanilla wafers = 1 cup crumbs
Chocolate:	1 ounce = 1 square baking (semi- or unsweetened)
Chocolate chips:	6 ounce pkg. = 1 cup
Cocoa:	1 pound = 4 cups ground chocolate
Almonds (unshelled):	1 pound = 1½ cups nutmeats
Pecans (unshelled):	1 pound = 2¼ cups nutmeats
Walnuts (unshelled):	1 pound = 2 cups nutmeats

Substitutions

BAKING AND COOKING INGREDIENTS:

<u>Baking powder</u> - for 1 teaspoon, substitute 1/4 teaspoon baking soda plus 5/8 teaspoon cream of tartar.

<u>Cream of tartar</u> - for 1/2 teaspoon, substitute 1½ teaspoons lemon juice, or vinegar.

<u>Cake flour</u> - for 1 cup, substitute 7/8 cup all-purpose flour.

Chocolate, Unsweetened - for 1 ounce, substitute 3 tablespoons cocoa plus 1 tablespoon fat (shortening or butter).

Chocolate, Semisweet - for 1 2/3 ounces, substitute 1 ounce unsweetened chocolate plus 4 teaspoons sugar.

Cornstarch (for thickening) - for 1 tablespoon, substitute approximately 2 tablespoons flour.

Corn syrup - for 1 cup, substitute 1 cup sugar mixed with 1/4 cup water or 1 cup honey.

Flour - for 1 tablespoon flour (as a thickener), substitute 1½ teaspoons cornstarch.

Honey - for 1 cup, substitute 1¼ cups sugar plus 1/4 cup water.

Molasses - for 1 cup, substitute 3/4 cup sugar plus 2 teaspoons baking powder (increase liquid called for in recipe by 5 tablespoons and decrease baking soda called for by 1/2 teaspoon) or 3/4 cup sugar plus 1¼ teaspoons cream of tartar (increase liquid called for in recipe by 5 tablespoons). You can also use an equivalent amount of honey as a replacement.

Shortening - for 1 cup melted, substitute 1 cup cooking oil. For 1 cup solid, substitute 1 cup butter; decrease salt in recipe by 1/2 teaspoon.

Sugar - for 1 cup, substitute 1 3/4 cups confectioner sugar, 1 cup firmly packed brown sugar, or 3/4 cup honey.

Sugar, Brown - for 1 cup firmly packed, substitute 1 cup granulated or 1 cup granulated plus 1/4 cup molasses.

Sugar, Confectioners - for 1 cup, substitute 3/4 cup granulated sugar.

Tapioca (as thickener in pies) - for 1 tablespoon, substitute 1 tablespoon flour.

DAIRY:

Eggs - for 1 egg, substitute 2 egg yolks plus 1 tablespoon water for baked goods; 2 egg yolks for custards and such mixtures.

Egg wash - use soy milk for a vegan substitute for egg wash called for in recipes such as on crusts or pastries.

Cream, Heavy - for 1 cup, substitute 3/4 cup milk plus 1/3 cup butter.

Cream, Sour - for 1 cup, substitute 7/8 cup buttermilk or 1 cup unflavored yogurt.

Cream, Whipped - for 1 cup whipping cream, substitute 1 cup evaporated milk that has been chilled at least 12 hours. Add 2 tablespoons sugar and 2 tablespoons lemon juice and beat until stiff.

Milk, Fresh whole - for 1 cup, substitute 1/2 cup evaporated plus 1/2 cup water or 1 cup reconstituted nonfat dry milk plus 2 tablespoons butter.

Milk, Sour or Buttermilk - for 1 cup, substitute 1 scant cup whole or skimmed milk plus 1 tablespoon vinegar or lemon juice or 1 3/4 teaspoons cream of tartar.

Yogurt - for 1 cup, substitute 1 cup buttermilk, 1 cup sour cream, or 1 cup cottage cheese blended until smooth.

FRUITS, VEGETABLES AND HERBS:

Bell pepper - for 1/2 cup diced fresh, substitute 1/4 cup bell pepper flakes.

Dry mustard - for 1 teaspoon, substitute 1 tablespoon prepared mustard.

Fresh herbs - for 2 to 3 tablespoons minced, substitute 1/2 teaspoon dry, 1/4 teaspoon if powdered form.

Garlic - for 1 clove, substitute 1/8 teaspoon garlic powder; for 1/2 teaspoon minced, substitute 1/4 teaspoon instant minced garlic.

Ginger - for a teaspoon chopped fresh, substitute 1/4 teaspoon ground ginger.

Grated fresh lemon or orange peel - for 1 teaspoon, substitute 1 teaspoon dried peel or 1/2 teaspoon lemon or orange extract.

Onion - for 1/3 cup chopped, substitute 1/4 cup dehydrated onion flakes.

Parsley - for 1/2 to 1 cup fresh, substitute 1/4 cup dehydrated parsley flakes.

Tomatoes, Canned - for 1 cup canned, substitute 1 1/3 cups cut-up fresh tomatoes, simmered 10 minutes.

Tomatoes, Fresh - for 2 cups fresh, substitute 1 16-ounce can, drained.

Tomato juice - for 1 cup, substitute 1/2 cup tomato sauce plus 1/2 cup water.

Tomato sauce - for 2 cups, substitute 3/4 cup tomato paste plus 1 cup water.

CONDIMENTS:

Catsup - for 1 cup, use 1 cup tomato sauce, 1/2 cup sugar, and 2 tablespoons vinegar. Mix well.

Chili sauce - for 1 cup, use 1 cup tomato sauce, 1/4 cup brown sugar, 2 tablespoons vinegar, 1/4 teaspoon cinnamon, and a dash of ground cloves and allspice.

Mayonnaise - for 1 cup, substitute 1 cup yogurt, sour cream, or cottage cheese puréed in blender. Use for all or part of mayonnaise called for in recipe.

The Well-Stocked Pantry

Having a well-stocked pantry makes meal preparation much easier. Here are a few basics you might want to keep on hand.

OILS

Canola oil is a neutral tasting oil, good for most recipes. Its high smoke point makes it good for frying. It is best kept in the refrigerator. Expeller pressed (process that extracts oil from seeds and nuts) oil is better tasting and healthier than oil processed by heat or chemicals.

Olive oil has great flavor and is mono-saturated, meaning it is heart healthy. It has a low smoke point, so it is best not to use it for high heat cooking. You will want to taste the oil to make sure it is fresh. Again, expeller pressed will taste better. Extra virgin generally is best for non-cooking applications, but again your own taste preference should guide you. Buy small quantities and keep in a dark cool space, but not the refrigerator.

Peanut oil has a nice nutty flavor and is good for frying, because it has a high smoke point. Keep it in the refrigerator.

Grapeseed oil is fairly neutral in flavor and has a high smoke point. Again, expeller pressed will be the best tasting.

Sesame oil is usually used as a garnish or in Asian dishes. It is highly flavorful, so a few drops are all you will need. It is very perishable, so always check for rancidity before using. Store it in the refrigerator.

SPICES AND HERBS

Most people buy spices and herbs in jars at the supermarket and keep them far too long. Spices and herbs deteriorate fairly quickly and most should be replaced after a year. It is much less expensive to buy small quantities of bulk spices and herbs in a store with high turnover and replace them every few months. Always smell and taste dried spices and herbs for freshness.

CANNED AND DRIED GOODS

It is a good idea to keep some canned and dried items in your pantry. Here are a few to consider.

Canned tomatoes are essential! Muir organic brand is consistent and comes in a variety of types and flavors. I particularly like the fire-roasted tomatoes.

Tomato paste in a tube will ensure that you don't waste a whole can when you just need a tablespoon.

Tuna is good for both salads and pasta dishes. Make sure it is sustainably harvested to ensure future fish stocks.

Rice in several varieties is good. It keeps well on the shelf, but you may want to store brown rice in the refrigerator.

Bulgur and quinoa are quick cooking and nutritious.

Pasta in several shapes will provide you with a fast weeknight meal. De Cecco brand has very good flavor. Always salt your cooking water generously!

Olives are great for snacks and can be a quick appetizer when paired with crackers, nuts and a nice cheese.

Beans are invaluable! Keep a selection of both canned and dried on hand. I like to control the salt by cooking dried beans and putting them in the freezer for future use.

Vinegars are great salt free flavor enhancers. I keep rice, sherry, apple cider, balsamic, and champagne vinegars, but choose the ones you like and use them in dressings, soups, pastas, and salads.

Salt is critical in the kitchen. There are many tasty choices, but always have coarse or kosher salt and fine table salt in your cupboard.

Consider investing in a good pepper mill and whole peppercorns. Freshly ground black pepper is far superior to pre-ground and is less expensive.

Good quality canned fruit is surprisingly good. Keep some pears and pineapple on hand for a quick dessert. Get the low sugar canned in juice style.

Always have fresh garlic and onions on hand and never store them in the refrigerator. If your garlic starts to sprout, cut it in half length-wise and remove the inner green part which is very bitter.

Low sodium chicken and vegetable broth is wonderful to have available.

Peanut butter & dried fruit for both snacking and cooking.

Index ~ Recipes by Garden Ingredient

Apples & Pears	Apples with Wild Rice & Almonds	147
	Apple-Stuffed Acorn Squash	98
	Best Sauerkraut Ever!	54
	Braised Red Cabbage	48
	Country-Style Skillet Apples	148
	Creamy Butternut Squash, Carrot, & Apple Soup	99
	Fresh Fruit Tarts	150
	Homemade Applesauce	149
	Irish Parsnip & Apple Soup	15
	Macerated Fruit Salad	148
	Maple Dressed Spinach Salad	138
	Old-Fashioned Baked Apples	148
	Poached Pears	149
	Spinach & Pear Salad	137
	Wild Bird Garland Treats	176
Artichokes	Artichoke Linguine	126
Asparagus	Asparagus, Spinach, & Strawberry Salad	89
	Asparagus with Balsamic Tomatoes	89
	Roasted Asparagus with Orange Sauce	90
	Sesame-Ginger Glazed Asparagus	90
Beets	Arugula & Beet Salad	136
	Beets in Mustard Vinaigrette	25
	Greens with Roasted Beets Salad	144
	Roasted Beet Salad with Oranges	24
	Roasted Beets	24
	Spoon Salad	45
Berries & Cherries	Asparagus, Spinach, & Strawberry Salad	89
	Berry Herbal Tea	158
	Berry Parfaits	157
	Blueberry & Corn Salad	154
	Blueberry Salsa	154
	Blueberry Tart	156

Berries & Cherries	Cherry Clafoutis	150
	Cranberry & Popcorn Bird Treats	176
	Easy Mixed Berry Smoothie	158
	Fresh Fruit Tarts	150
	Frozen Strawberry Jam	152
	Macerated Fruit Salad	148
	Minted Blackberry Ice Tea	159
	Mixed Berry Compote	155
	Raspberry Bread Pudding	151
	Raspberry Sauce	150
	Strawberry Glacé Pie	153
	Strawberry Icebox Pie	152
	Strawberry Sauce	154
	Very Berry Lemonade	157
	Wild Bird Garland Treats	176
Bok Choy	Summer Vegetable Stir-Fry	53
Broccoli	Broccoli Florets with Lemon Butter Sauce	34
	Broccoli Gratin	35
	Broccoli Quiche	32
	Broccoli Stuffed Potatoes	34
	Roasted Brassicas	35
	Summer Vegetable Stir-Fry	53
	The Best Ever Vegan "Macaroni & Cheese"	36
Brussels Sprouts	Brussels Sprouts Salad	37
	Brussels Sprouts with Caramelized Onions	39
	Savory Brussels Sprouts Hash	38
Cabbage	Best Sauerkraut Ever!	54
	Bonnie's Cabbage Salad	49
	Braised Red Cabbage	48
	Fennel, Cabbage, & Carrot Slaw	92
	Garden Vegetable Minestrone Soup	113
	Irish Potato & Leek Soup	18
	Jalapeño Slaw	49
	Koldermer, Lazy Style	51
	Rumblededumps	52

Cabbage	Spoon Salad	45
	Sweet-Sour Red Cabbage	48
	Veggie Pancakes	52
	Wasabi Slaw	50
Carrots	Bonnie's Cabbage Salad	49
	Carrot Cookies	13
	Carrot Loaf	14
	Carrot Orzo	11
	Creamy Butternut Squash, Carrot, & Apple Soup	99
	Creamy Carrot Soup	10
	Fennel, Cabbage, & Carrot Slaw	92
	Garden Vegetable Minestrone Soup	113
	Hearty Vegetable Roast	25
	Homemade Vegetable Stock	31
	Jalapeño Slaw	49
	Kale & Potato Soup	44
	Orange-Roasted Carrots	12
	Oven-Roasted Carrots & Potatoes	12
	Parsnip & Carrot Bake	14
	Pickled Vegetables	30
	Roasted Fennel & Carrots	91
	Roasted Vegetable Ragout	26
	Roasted Vegetables with Chimichurri Sauce	28
	Root Vegetable Pot Pie	27
	Rumblededumps	52
	Sautéed Carrots	11
	Sautéed Zucchini & Carrot Ribbons	111
	Snow Pea Stir-Fry	63
	Spoon Salad	45
	Summer Vegetable Pot Pie	71
	Summer Vegetable Stir-Fry	53
	Vegetable & Barley Soup	70
	Vegetable Chili	128
	Veggie Pancakes	52
	Wasabi Slaw	50

Carrots	White Bean Stew	127
	Zucchini & Carrot Casserole	113
Cauliflower	Cauliflower "Mashed Potatoes"	37
	Deep Fried Cauliflower	36
	Fennel & Cauliflower Gratin	93
	Pickled Vegetables	30
	Roasted Brassicas	35
	Tangy Mustard Cauliflower	38
Chard	Bacon & Swiss Chard Pasta	142
	Baked Sausage, Chard, & Penne Pasta	142
	Brussels Sprouts Salad	37
	Easy Spinach Lasagna Roll-ups	140
	Garlicky Swiss Chard & Beans	141
	Spoon Salad	45
Corn	Blueberry & Corn Salad	154
	Confetti Peppers & Corn	124
	Corn & Potato Chowder	59
	Corn Pudding	60
	Corn in the Husks	58
	Jalapeño Corn Cakes	61
	Summer Succotash Salad	58
	Summer Vegetable Pasta	112
	Summer Vegetable Pot Pie	71
	Tex-Mex Tortillas Soup	129
	Zucchini-Corn Casserole	110
Cucumber	Blueberry & Corn Salad	154
	Bread & Butter Pickles	134
	Creamy Cucumber Salad	116
	Cucumber Salad	116
	Easy Gazpacho	123
	"Lime" Sweet Pickles	132
	Mediterranean Chopped Salad	122
	Mediterranean Spinach & Rice Salad	139
	Refrigerator Dills	134
	Quinoa Salad	79

Cucumber	Tomato Lentil Salad	122
Dried Beans, Peas, & Grains	Ancient Grains Polenta with Puttanesca Sauce	80
	Bean Soup	75
	Butternut Squash "Lasagna"	100
	Caribbean Bean Soup	146
	Cedars-Inspired Lentil Soup	78
	Chocolate Peanut Butter Pie with Teff Crust	84
	Dried Bean Soup	76
	Fennel Mediterranean Salad	91
	Flourless Pancakes	86
	Garden Vegetable Minestrone Soup	113
	Garlicky Swiss Chard & Beans	141
	Gluten Free Whole Grain Muffins	86
	Herby White Bean Spread	169
	Indian Greens & Garbanzos	143
	Lentil & Quinoa Breakfast Patties	82, 101
	Mushroom & Barley Soup with Collard Greens	145
	Oatcakes	83
	Polenta with Butter & Cheese	82
	Polish Mushroom & Barley Christmas Soup	76
	Quinoa Salad	79
	Roasted Vegetables with Chimichurri Sauce	28
	Squash with Kale & Beans	102
	Summer Succotash	58
	Sweet Potato Hummus	22
	Tabbouleh	77
	Tex-Mex Tortillas Soup	129
	Tomato Lentil Salad	122
	Vegetable & Barley Soup	70
	Vegetable Chili	128
	White Bean Stew	127
Eggplant	Eggplant & Squash Ratatouille	124
	Stacked Eggplant Parmesan	126
Fennel	Fennel & Cauliflower Gratin	93
	Fennel Mediterranean Salad	91

Fennel	Fennel Slaw with Orange Vinaigrette	92
	Fennel, Cabbage & Carrot Slaw	92
	Hearty Vegetable Roast	25
	Roasted Fennel & Carrots	91
	Roasted Vegetable Ragout	26
	Roasted Vegetables with Chimichurri Sauce	28
Garlic	Roasted Garlic	31
Green Beans	Dilly Bean Potato Salad	66
	Dilly Beans in a Hurry	67
	Dilly Beans	66
	Herbed Green Beans	65
	Marinated Green Bean & Potato Salad	68
	Mustardy Green & Yellow Beans	70
	Oven-roasted Green Beans	65
	Pesto Pasta with Green Beans & Potatoes	69
	Pickled Vegetables	30
	Schnittbohnensalat ~ German Green Bean Salad	68
	Summer Vegetable Pot Pie	71
Greens	Arugula & Beet Salad	136
	Baby Greens with Balsamic Vinaigrette	135
	Caribbean Bean Soup	146
	Flowery Greens	164
	Fresh Greens with Thyme Dressing	163
	Greens with Roasted Beets Salad	144
	Greens, Beets & Toasted Walnut Salad	144
	Indian Greens & Garbanzos	143
	Mushroom & Barley Soup with Fresh Collards	145
	Pea Pod Salad with Ginger Dressing	62
	Peppery Mustard Greens Salad	136
	Watercress & Radish Salad	137
Herbs & Flowers	Aromatic Kitchen Hot Pads	176
	Basic Herbal Vinegar	174
	Brined Sunflower Seeds	160
	Flowery Greens	164
	Fresh Greens with Thyme Dressing	163

Herbs & Flowers	Fresh Herb Mayonnaise	170
	Green Rice Pilaf	164
	Herb & Yogurt Dressing	171
	Herb Bath Sachets	174
	Herbal Honey	171
	Herbal Oil	173
	Herbal Sachets	176
	Herbal Soap	175
	Herbal Tea	172
	Herbed Biscuits	168
	Herbed Cheese Spread	168
	Herbed French Dressing	171
	Herbed Salt	172
	Herby Green Beans	165
	Herby White Bean Spread	169
	Lavender Shortbread	172
	Lemony Nasturtium Butter	170
	Linda's TJ Dilly Bread	165
	Moth-proof Sachets	176
	Nasturtium Vinegar	171
	Pesto Sauce	170
	Potpourri	175
	Rosemary Focaccia Bread	166
	Rosemary Oil	173
	Rosewater	175
	Simple Herb Butter	169
	Soft Herb Rolls	166
	Sunflower Backyard Bird Treat	176
Kale	Bean Soup	75
	Crispy Kale	46
	Egg, Kale & Ricotta on Toast	45
	Homemade Bibimbap	47
	Kale & Potato Soup	44
	Kale, Potato & Sausage Casserole	46
	Kale & Raisin Pasta	43

Kale	Kale Salad with Nuts & Dried Fruit	42
	Kale with Garlic & Thyme	41
	North African Stew	23
	Roasted Vegetables with Chimichurri Sauce	28
	Slathered Kale Slaw	41
	Spoon Salad	45
	Squash with Kale & Beans	102
Kohlrabi	Simple Kohlrabi Salad	40
	Parmesan Kohlrabi	40
Leeks	Irish Potato & Leek Soup	18
	Parmesan Kohlrabi	40
	Root Vegetable Pot Pie	27
	Zucchini "Vichyssoise"	108
Lettuce	*See Greens*	
Lima Beans	Lima Beans with Pancetta	69
Onions	Brussels Sprouts with Caramelized Onions	39
	Hearty Vegetable Roast	25
	Homemade Vegetable Stock	31
	Pickled Red Onions	30
	Roasted Vegetable Ragout	26
Parsnips	Hearty Vegetable Roast	25
	Irish Parsnip & Apple Soup	15
	Parsnip & Carrot Bake	14
	Parsnip Purée	15
	Roasted Vegetable Ragout	26
	Roasted Vegetables with Chimichurri Sauce	28
	Root Vegetable Pot Pie	27
Peas, Shelled	Minted Sweet Peas	63
	Pea Spaetzle	64
	Summer Vegetable Pot Pie	71
Peas, Snap, & Snow	Citrusy Pea Pod Salad	62
	Pea Pod Salad with Ginger Dressing	62
	Pea Pods in Orange Sauce	61
	Quick & Easy Snow Pea Salad	64
	Roasted Snap Peas	63

Peas, Snap & Snow	Snow Pea Stir-Fry	63
	Summer Vegetable Stir-Fry	53
Peppers	Avocado, Onion & Pepper Salad	124
	Blueberry & Corn Salad	154
	Blueberry Salsa	154
	Bonnie's Cabbage Salad	49
	Caribbean Bean Soup	146
	Confetti Peppers & Corn	124
	Corn Pudding	70
	Cucumber Salad	116
	Easy Gazpacho	123
	Eggplant & Squash Ratatouille	124
	Fresh Tomato Salsa	120
	Jalapeño Corn Cakes	61
	Jalapeño Slaw	49
	Mediterranean Chopped Salad	122
	Mediterranean Spinach & Rice Salad	139
	Mexicali Rice	123
	Quick & Easy Snow Pea Salad	64
	Quinoa Salad	79
	Roasted Vegetable Ragout	26
	Summer Succotash Salad	58
	Summer Vegetable Pot Pie	71
	Tex-Mex Tortillas Soup	129
	Tomato Lentil Salad	122
	Vegetable & Barley Soup	70
	Vegetable Chili	128
	Wasabi Slaw	50
	Zucchini-Corn Casserole	110
Potatoes	Broccoli Stuffed Potatoes	34
	Corn & Potato Chowder	69
	Cumin Potato Salad	17
	Dilly Bean Potato Salad	66
	Easy Roast Yellow Potatoes	16
	Fingerling Potatoes with Rosemary	18

Potatoes	Hearty Vegetable Roast	25
	Irish Potato & Leek Soup	18
	Kale & Potato Soup	44
	Kale, Potato, & Sausage Casserole	46
	Marinated Green Bean & Potato Salad	68
	Old-Fashioned Potato Bread	19
	Oven-Roasted Carrots & Potatoes	12
	Pesto Pasta with Green Beans & Potatoes	69
	Potato & Turnip Gratin	20
	Roasted Potato Medley	20
	Root Vegetable Pot Pie	27
	Rosemary New Potatoes	17
	Rumblededumps	52
	Sage Roasted Potatoes	16
	Zucchini "Vichyssoise"	108
Pumpkin	Creamy Pumpkin Risotto	104
	Pumpkin Bread	107
	Pumpkin Caraway Soup	106
	Spiced Pumpkin Seeds	159
	Squash Dinner Rolls	104
Radish	Cucumber Salad	116
	Watercress & Radish Salad	137
Rhubarb	Rhubarb Cookies	96
	Rhubarb Crumble	94
	Rhubarb Marmalade	97
	Rhubarb Muffins	95
	Rhubarb Sauce	97
	Rhubarb Walnut Bread	94
Rutabaga	Hearty Vegetable Roast	25
	Potato & Turnip Gratin	20
Seeds	Backyard Birds Treat	174
	Brined Sunflower Seeds	160
	Spiced Pumpkin Seeds	159
Snow & Snap Peas	*See Peas*	
Spinach	Asparagus, Spinach, & Strawberry Salad	89

Spinach	Citrusy Pea Pod Salad	62
	Creamed Spinach	140
	Easy Spinach Lasagna Roll-ups	140
	Maple Dressed Spinach Salad	138
	Mediterranean Spinach & Rice Salad	139
	Spinach & Pear Salad	137
	Spinach Rigatoni	138
Squash	*See Winter Squash; Zucchini & Summer Squash*	
Sweet Potatoes & Yams	Carolyn's Roasted Sweet Potatoes	21
	Cheesy Sweet Potato Mash	21
	Hearty Vegetable Roast	25
	North African Stew	23
	Roasted Potato Medley	20
	Roasted Vegetables with Chimichurri Sauce	28
	Sweet Potato Hummus	22
Tomatoes	Asparagus with Balsamic Tomatoes	89
	Baked Sausage, Chard, & Penne Pasta	142
	Basic Fresh Tomato Sauce	130
	Butternut Squash "Lasagna"	100
	Crusty Broiled Tomatoes	118
	Easy Gazpacho	123
	Easy Tomato Sauce	2, 130
	Eggplant & Squash Ratatouille	124
	Fennel Mediterranean Salad	91
	Fresh Tomato Pasta	120
	Fresh Tomato Salsa	120
	Garden Vegetable Minestrone Soup	113
	Make It Yourself Catsup	131
	Mediterranean Chopped Salad	122
	Mexicali Rice	123
	Nana's Tomato Salad	117
	Oven-Dried Tomatoes	118
	Pasta Amatriciana	121
	Plum Tomato Chutney	132
	Puttanesca Sauce	81

Tomatoes	Roasted Tomatoes	119
	Sautéed Zucchini & Tomatoes	110
	Spinach Rigatoni	138
	Summer Vegetable Pasta	112
	Tex-Mex Tortillas Soup	129
	Tomato & Bread Salad ~ Panzanella	117
	Tomato & Olive Bruschetta	119
	Tomato Lentil Salad	122
	Vegetable & Barley Soup	70
	White Bean Stew	127
Turnips	Hearty Vegetable Roast	25
	Potato & Turnip Gratin	20
Watercress	Dilly Bean Potato Salad	66
	Spoon Salad	45
	Watercress & Radish Salad	137
Winter Squash	Apple-Stuffed Acorn Squash	98
	Butternut Squash "Lasagna"	100
	Butternut Squash Dumplings	103
	Caribbean Bean Soup	146
	Creamy Butternut Squash, Carrot, & Apple Soup	99
	Hearty Vegetable Roast	25
	Squash Dinner Rolls	104
	Squash with Kale & Beans	102
Zucchini & Summer Squash	Chilled Zucchini Soup with Cilantro Cream	109
	Eggplant & Squash Ratatouille	124
	Garden Vegetable Minestrone Soup	113
	Roasted Vegetable Ragout	26
	Sautéed Zucchini & Carrot Ribbons	111
	Sautéed Zucchini & Tomatoes	110
	Spoon Salad	45
	Summer Vegetable Pasta	112
	Summer Vegetable Pot Pie	71
	Vegetable & Barley Soup	70
	Vegetable Chili	128
	Wild Bird Garland Treats	176

Zucchini & Summer Squash	Zucchini "Lasagna"	108
	Zucchini "Vichyssoise"	108
	Zucchini & Carrot Casserole	113
	Zucchini Bread	114
	Zucchini Cakes	111
	Zucchini Hummus	107
	Zucchini-Corn Casserole	11

Index ~ Recipes by Meal Item

Appetizers, Snacks & Spreads	Blueberry Salsa	154
	Brined Sunflower Seeds	160
	Crispy Kale	46
	Deep Fried Cauliflower	36
	Dilly Beans	66
	Dilly Beans in a Hurry	67
	Fresh Tomato Salsa	120
	Herbed Cheese Spread	168
	Herby White Bean Spread	169
	Oven-Dried Tomatoes	118
	Roasted Garlic	31
	Spiced Pumpkin Seeds	159
	Sweet Potato Hummus	22
	Tomato & Olive Bruschetta	119
	Zucchini Hummus	107
Beverages	Berry Herbal Tea	158
	Herbal Tea	172
	Easy Mixed Berry Smoothie	158
	Minted Blackberry Ice Tea	159
	Very Berry Lemonade	157
Bread	Carrot Loaf	14
	Gluten Free Whole Grain Muffins	86
	Herbed Biscuits	168
	Homemade Croutons	120
	Linda's TJ Dilly Bread	165
	Old-Fashioned Potato Bread	19
	Pot Pie Biscuits	72
	Pumpkin Bread	107
	Rhubarb Muffins	95
	Rhubarb Walnut Bread	94
	Rosemary Focaccia Bread	166
	Soft Herb Rolls	166

Bread	Squash Dinner Rolls	104
	Zucchini Bread	114
Condiments & Flavorings	Basic Herbal Vinegar	174
	Bread & Butter Pickles	134
	Country-Style Skillet Apples	148
	Fresh Herb Mayonnaise	170
	Herbal Honey	171
	Herbal Oil	173
	Herbed Salt	172
	Homemade Applesauce	149
	Homemade Croutons	120
	Lemony Nasturtium Butter	170
	"Lime" Sweet Pickles	132
	Make It Yourself Catsup	131
	Mixed Berry Compote	155
	Nasturtium Vinegar	171
	Oven-Dried Tomatoes	118
	Plum Tomato Chutney	132
	Refrigerator Dills	143
	Roasted Garlic	31
	Roasted Tomatoes	119
	Rosemary Oil	173
	Rosewater	175
	Simple Herb Butter	169
Desserts & Sweets	Berry Parfaits	157
	Blueberry Tart	156
	Carrot Cookies	13
	Cherry Clafoutis	150
	Chocolate Peanut Better Pie with Teff Crust	84
	Coconut Whipped Cream	85
	Fresh Fruit Tarts	150
	Lavender Shortbread	172
	Mom's Pie Crust	28, 33, 153
	Old-fashioned Baked Apples	148
	Poached Pears	149

Desserts & Sweets	Raspberry Bread Pudding	151
	Rhubarb Cookies	96
	Rhubarb Crumble	94
	Strawberry Glace' Pie	153
	Strawberry Icebox Pie	152
Dressings & Sauces	Avocado Chimichurri Sauce	29
	Basic Fresh Tomato Sauce	130
	Easy Tomato Sauce	102, 130
	Fresh Greens with Thyme Dressing	163
	Herb & Yogurt Dressing	171
	Herbed French Dressing	171
	Pesto Sauce	170
	Puttanesca Sauce	81
	Raspberry Sauce	150
	Rhubarb Sauce	97
	Strawberry Sauce	154
Main Dishes	Artichoke Linguine	126
	Bacon & Swiss Chard Pasta	142
	Baked Sausage, Chard & Penne Pasta	142
	Broccoli Quiche	32
	Broccoli Stuffed Potatoes	34
	Butternut Squash "Lasagna"	100
	Carrot Orzo	11
	Creamy Pumpkin Risotto	104
	Easy Spinach Lasagna Roll-ups	140
	Egg, Kale & Ricotta on Toast	45
	Eggplant & Squash Ratatouille	124
	Flourless Pancakes	86
	Fresh Tomato Pasta	120
	Garlicky Swiss Chard & Beans	141
	Hearty Vegetable Roast	25
	Homemade Bibimbap	47
	Indian Greens & Garbanzos	143
	Kale & Raisin Pasta	43
	Kale, Potato & Sausage Casserole	46

Main Dishes	Koldermer, Lazy Style	51
	Lentil & Quinoa Breakfast Patties	82, 101
	Pasta Amatriciana	121
	Pea Spaetzle	64
	Pasta with Green Beans & Potatoes	69
	Roasted Vegetable Ragout	26
	Roasted Vegetables with Chimichurri Sauce	28
	Root Vegetable Pot Pie	27
	Rumblededumps	52
	Snow Pea Stir-Fry	63
	Spinach Rigatoni	138
	Stacked Eggplant Parmesan	126
	Summer Vegetable Pasta	112
	Summer Vegetable Pot Pie	71
	Summer Vegetable Stir-Fry	53
	The Best Ever Vegan "Macaroni & Cheese"	36
	Vegetable Chili	128
	Zucchini & Carrot Casserole	113
	Zucchini Cakes	111
	Zucchini-Corn Casserole	110
	Zucchini "Lasagna"	108
Pickles & Preserves	Best Ever Sauerkraut!	54
	Bread & Butter Pickles	134
	Dilly Beans	66
	Dilly Beans in as Hurry	67
	Frozen Strawberry Jam	152
	"Lime" Sweet Pickles	132
	Pickled Red Onions	30
	Pickled Vegetables	30
	Refrigerator Dills	134
	Rhubarb Marmalade	97
Salads	Arugula & Beet Salad	136
	Asparagus, Spinach & Strawberry Salad	89
	Avocado, Onion & Pepper Salad	124
	Baby Greens with Balsamic Vinaigrette	135

Salads

Recipe	Page
Blueberry & Corn Salad	154
Bonnie's Cabbage Salad	49
Brussels Sprouts Salad	37
Citrusy Pea Pod Salad	62
Creamy Cucumber Salad	116
Cucumber Salad	116
Cumin Potato Salad	17
Dilly Bean Potato Salad	66
Fennel Mediterranean Salad	91
Fennel Slaw with Orange Vinaigrette	92
Fennel, Cabbage & Carrot Slaw	92
Fresh Greens with Thyme Dressing	163
Flowery Greens	164
Greens with Roasted Beets Salad	144
Greens, Beets & Toasted Walnut Salad	144
Jalapeño Slaw	49
Kale Salad with Nuts & Dried Fruit	42
Macerated Fruit Salad	148
Maple Dressed Spinach Salad	138
Marinated Green Bean & Potato Salad	68
Mediterranean Chopped Salad	122
Mediterranean Spinach and Rice Salad	139
Nana's Tomato Salad	117
Pea Pod Salads with Ginger Dressing	62
Peppery Mustard Greens Salad	136
Quick & Easy Snow Pea Salad	64
Quinoa Salad	79
Roasted Beet Salad with Oranges	24
Schnittbohnensalat ~ German Green Bean Salad	68
Simple Kohlrabi Salad	40
Slathered Kale Slaw	41
Spinach & Pear Salad	137
Spoon Salad	45
Summer Succotash Salad	58
Tabbouleh	77

Salads	Tomato & Bread Salad ~ Panzanella	117
	Tomato Lentil Salad	122
	Wasabi Slaw	50
	Watercress & Radish Salad	137
Main Dishes, Side Dishes <u>or</u> Vegetarian		
	Ancient Grains Polenta with Puttanesca Sauce	80
	Apples with Wild Rice & Almonds	147
	Apple-Stuffed Acorn Squash	98
	Asparagus with Balsamic Tomatoes	89
	Beets in Mustard Vinaigrette	25
	Braised Red Cabbage	48
	Broccoli Florets with Lemon Butter Sauce	34
	Broccoli Gratin	35
	Broccoli Stuffed Potatoes	34
	Brussels Sprouts with Caramelized Onions	39
	Butternut Squash Dumplings	103
	Carolyn's Roasted Sweet Potatoes	21
	Cauliflower "Mashed Potatoes"	37
	Cheesy Sweet Potato Mash	21
	Confetti Peppers & Corn	124
	Corn Pudding	60
	Creamed Spinach	140
	Crusty Broiled Tomatoes	118
	Easy Roasted Yellow Potatoes	16
	Fennel & Cauliflower Gratin	93
	Fingerling Potatoes with Rosemary	18
	Green Rice Pilaf	164
	Grilled Corn in the Husks	58
	Herbed Green Beans	65
	Herby Green Beans	165
	Jalapeño Corn Cakes	61
	Kale with Garlic & Thyme	41
	Lima Beans with Pancetta	69
	Mexicali Rice	123
	Minted Sweet Peas	63

Main Dishes, Side Dishes <u>or</u> Vegetarian	Mustardy Green & Yellow Beans	70
	Oatcakes	83
	Oven-Roasted Carrots & Potatoes	12
	Oven-Roasted Carrots	12
	Oven-Roasted Green Beans	65
	Parmesan Kohlrabi	40
	Parsnip & Carrot Bake	14
	Parsnip Purée	15
	Sautéed Zucchini & Carrot Ribbons	111
	Sautéed Zucchini & Tomatoes	110
	Savory Brussels Sprouts Hash	38
	Snow Pea Stir-Fry	63
	Squash with Kale & Beans	102
	Sweet-Sour Cabbage	48
	Tangy Mustard Cauliflower	38
	Veggie Pancakes	52
Soups & Stews	Bean Soup	75
	Caribbean Bean Soup	146
	Cedars-Inspired Lentil Soup	78
	Chilled Zucchini Soup with Cilantro Cream	109
	Corn & Potato Chowder	59
	Creamy Butternut, Carrot & Apple Soup	99
	Creamy Carrot Soup	10
	Dried Bean Soup	76
	Easy Gazpacho	123
	Garden Vegetable Minestrone Soup	113
	Homemade Vegetable Stock	31
	Irish Parsnip & Apple Soup	15
	Irish Potato & Leek Soup	18
	Kale & Potato Soup	44
	Mushroom & Barley Soup with Fresh Collard Greens	145
	North African Stew	23
	Polish Mushroom & Barley Christmas Soup	76

Soups & Stews	Pumpkin Caraway Soup	106
	Tex-Mex Tortilla Soup	129
	Vegetable & Barley Soup	70
	Vegetable Chili	128
	White Bean Stew	127
	Zucchini "Vichyssoise"	108

GRUB
GARDEN-RAISED BOUNTY